KING'S CROSS TO POTTERS BAR

Charlie and Jim Connor

Series editor Vic Mitchell

MP Middleton Press

Front cover photograph : Sir Nigel Gresley's record-breaking A4 Pacific No 60022 *Mallard*, is seen passing Harringay West on an up express in 1962. (D.I.D. Loveday / The Gresley Society)

Back cover : Commuters stream past 'Baby Deltic' No D5903, in two-tone green livery, as she stands beneath the trainshed roof at King's Cross during the second half of the 1960s. (J.E. Connor)

ISBN   978 1 906008 62 8

First published November 2009

© Middleton Press,

Published by
  Middleton Press
  Easebourne Lane
  Midhurst, West Sussex
  GU29 9AZ
Tel: 01730 813169
Fax: 01730 812601
Email : info@middletonpress.co.uk
www.middletonpress.co.uk

Layout and typesetting CDC design

Printed in the United Kingdom by Henry Ling Limited, at the Dorset Press, Dorchester, DT1 1HD

INDEX

GEOGRAPHICAL SETTING

When opened, King's Cross was on the northern fringe of urban London. The lines immediately pass under the Northern Heights in tunnels after leaving King's Cross. London Clay is the main underlying material, it being used for brickmaking during the development era.

The route is on a steady up gradient, apart from about one mile near Hornsey. Three tunnels north of there made this possible, Enfield Chase being the most notable ridge of high ground.

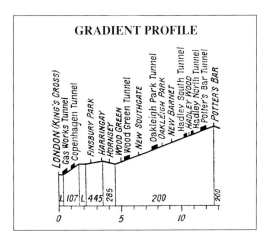

ACKNOWLEDGMENTS

We would like to thank all the photographers, without whose enthusiasm and interest in years gone by albums such as this could not have been produced. We also wish to express our gratitude to Peter Kay for his assistance and Geoff Goslin who allowed us access to his comprehensive collection of photographs.

Finally, mention must be made of the various company and Board of Trade files which are held at the National Archives, Kew. These provide the researcher with a wealth of facts and are an essential asset to all who are involved in the study of railway history.

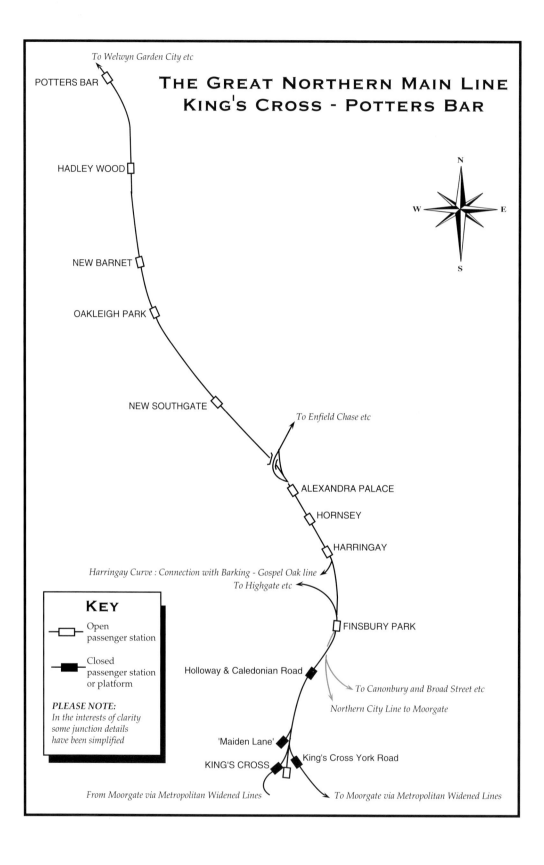

HISTORICAL BACKGROUND

In the spring of 1846, the Great Northern Railway presented a Bill to Parliament, requesting authority to construct a line between London and York. The proposal met with a certain amount of opposition, but this was soon overruled and the company's Act received the Royal Assent on 26th June 1846. Preliminary work was soon under way and, within a short while, the main works south of Peterborough could begin.

The line was to start from a terminus at King's Cross then head northwards through Holloway, Hornsey and East Barnet. The contract for much of the work was awarded to the well-known railway builder, Thomas Brassey, but soon after construction commenced, the scheme was threatened by financial problems. Brassey nevertheless continued and works were established along the route at Holloway, Potters Bar and Welwyn to supply the necessary bricks.

By the early months of 1848 there was a total of around 5,000 or 6,000 men employed on the project and work was progressing well. Engineering through the London clay south of Potters Bar was beset with difficulties however, as the builders had to provide five tunnels, of which the longest stretched for a length of 1,214 yards.

In 1849 contracts for the final mile into the London terminus were awarded to Pearce & Smith and John Jay, with the former being responsible for building Copenhagen Tunnel. By the summer of that year Brassey could confidently tell the Chief Engineer that all was well and only a few major engineering works were still outstanding. Unfortunately clearance of the King's Cross site proved to be protracted, so the company decided to construct a temporary terminus a little to the north at Maiden Lane.

Details regarding the siting of intermediate stations were not finalised until late 1849, but the company remained optimistic and were hoping that the route would open in May 1850. However in the February of that year it was stated that work remained to be done on Copenhagen Tunnel and the completion of Welwyn Viaduct had been delayed due to problems with frost. Added to this, a section of viaduct which was being built to carry today's North London Line above the GNR south of Copenhagen Tunnel

collapsed onto the works, but undeterred, the engineers carried on.

Eventually the route was ready for use and the section between Maiden Lane and Peterborough was opened to public traffic on 7th August 1850.

In the meantime, work had started on the final stretch into the permanent terminus, although very little could be done until a fever hospital occupying the site was closed and demolished. To accommodate the extension, a further tunnel was required as the route had to pass beneath the Regent's Canal. The arrangement called for some careful engineering and took time to complete, but within a couple of years King's Cross was ready to receive its first passengers.

The permanent station was a vast improvement over its temporary predeccessor and opened on 14th October 1852. Since then it has undergone numerous changes and details of these will be found within the pictorial section of this book.

In October 1863 a service was introduced linking the GNR with the Metropolitan Railway, by way of two new spurs at King's Cross. These lay either side of the terminus, with the down line to the west and the up to the east. Eleven years later a curve was brought into use which linked Finsbury Park with Canonbury on the North London Railway and provided a route into the NLR City terminus at Broad Street.

As the nineteenth century drew to a close, Parliamentary authority was given for another link at Finsbury Park, but this time it would take the form of a tube line into Moorgate. The company undertaking its construction was the Great Northern & City Railway and the route was to be enclosed for much of its length in twin tunnels, each with a diameter of 16ft. These were larger than those used on other tube lines because they were intended to accommodate standard height rolling stock. The line was to commence at at junction with the GNR and when complete, would allow through running to and from the northern suburbs. Because steam locomotives would not be permitted in the tubes, it was planned to change to electric traction at Finsbury Park, but in October 1900 the GNR cancelled its agreement regarding through running, and when the line opened in 1904, services operated in isolation. A later scheme to provide a link between the GNCR and the main line suburban system came to nothing and it would be many years before a physical connection materialised.

The GNR became part of the London & North Eastern Railway under the grouping of 1923 and was absorbed into the Eastern Region of British Railways in 1948 when the network was nationalised.

Throughout these years steam reigned supreme on all services, but changes were to come after diesel traction appeared during the second half of the 1950s. The following decade saw the eradication of regular steam working completely. The onset of the 'Corporate Image' period in 1964 and 1965, saw the title 'British Railways' being shortened to 'British Rail' and the adoption of a new 'double-arrow' symbol for branding purposes, but for a while at least the stations on the former Great Northern suburban system remained little altered. As the 1960s drew to a close however, their flaking paintwork and blue enamel nameboards emphasised that they were relics from a previous era and that change could not be far away.

These changes were to come in the 1970s, with the replacement of manual signal boxes by a new signalling centre at King's Cross and the promise of suburban electrification. The scheme, which was announced in the autumn of 1970, also included the rationalisation of existing trackwork and was estimated to cost £7.4million. Details of the electrification scheme emerged in 1971, with stage 1 covering the suburban routes to and from Hertford North and Welwyn Garden City. The plan also revived the idea of a connection with the ex-GNCR tube line at Finsbury Park, thereby ending its isolation. For many years the old GNCR, or 'Northern City Line' as it was known, had been part of the London Underground system, but this change would bring it firmly into the main line suburban network. The GN electrification was to be carried out using the 25kV overhead system, but the section through the tube tunnels would employ third rail owing to clearance difficulties.

In connection with these alterations, the passenger services linking the former GNR with the Metropolitan Widened Lines and Broad Street were withdrawn from 7th November 1976. Regular electric services linking Moorgate with Hertford North and Welwyn Garden City commenced on the following day, but electric trains connecting King's Cross with Stevenage, Hitchin, Letchworth, and Royston were not introduced until February 1978.

From 10th June 1986 the lines serving London and the Home Counties came under the banner of Network SouthEast, but continued to be part of British Rail. This arrangement subsequently ended when the country's unified railway system was broken up into privatised sectors, with the former GNR suburban services passing to West Anglia Great Northern from 5th January 1997. A further change came in April 2006, when a new franchise resulted in WAGN combining with Thameslink to form First Capital Connect.

PASSENGER SERVICES

Although space restrictions do not permit a detailed look at passenger services operating to and from King's Cross, there can be no doubt that the station and the East Coast Main Line in general have always been a prime asset to the British railway network.

To many, the route will always be associated with long-distance trains. Enthusiasts fondly recall the inter-war period when swish, streamlined expresses such as 'The Silver Jubilee' and 'The Coronation' conveyed their passengers in art-deco comfort between London and the north. Others look back on the famous locomotive classes; Stirling's 8ft singles, the Ivatt Atlantics, the Gresley Pacifics and the impressive Deltics. All of these have played their part in the history of King's Cross and there can be few amongst the railway fraternity who do not have a particular favourite.

During the 1920s and 30s, the glamour of the main line, with its record-breaking locomotives, contrasted sharply with the suburban services which plied back and forth between King's Cross and the dormitory towns of

Hertfordshire. Here the rolling-stock was often of the close-coupled four-coach articulated sets known as 'Quad-Arts', introduced during the Gresley era and still in service until being replaced by vehicles of BR design. Enthusiasts of a certain age will fondly remember the N2 class of 0-6-2T which worked these trains with such aplomb before they were made redundant by dieselisation. There was little doubt that these sturdy locomotives possessed character, but to travel behind one through the tunnels out of King's Cross could be a very sulphuric experience.

Suburban passenger services using the section of line between King's Cross and Potters Bar were those travelling to Hatfield, Welwyn Garden City and, for part of the distance at least, trains bound for the Hertford Loop. These diverged from the route at Wood Green and still do, although the station is now known as Alexandra Palace. To the historically minded this renaming perhaps seems confusing as until 1954 a completely different Alexandra Palace station was terminus of a branch line, which diverged at Highgate and served the area around Muswell Hill.

Trains working the old Alexandra Palace branch once used the main line, but they were subsequently cut back to start and terminate at Finsbury Park. Other Great Northern suburban branches, known collectively as 'the Northern Heights', were also served by trains from King's Cross, until the route leading to High Barnet and part of that into Edgware were transferred to the London Underground system in connection with the schemes announced in the mid-1930s.

Seeing how busy the line is today, it seems hard to believe that back in 1850 there were only eight trains in each direction serving Maiden Lane on weekdays, with three on Sundays. Things improved greatly in the following decades however, and King's Cross has subsequently seen so much traffic that a study of its passenger services would require a volume of its own. However some of the workings have been of a more unusual nature and these perhaps deserve a special mention.

Back in the 1850s, over a decade before St Pancras was opened, the Midland Railway was using the London & North Western station at Euston as its London terminus. The advent of a Midland line towards Hitchin however offered the possibility of an alternative route, so the company entered into negotiations with the GNR regarding the use of King's Cross. The talks did not run smoothly, but agreement was reached on 2nd December 1857, when the GNR accepted an annual sum of £1,500 for the use of its terminus. Midland trains began working into King's Cross from 1st February 1858 and although commercially successful, the increase in traffic on the line was soon causing problems. Delays became commonplace and the Midland sought powers to build its own line into London. A Bill was presented to Parliament and after much opposition was sanctioned in June 1863. When the final stretch into St Pancras was opened to passenger traffic on 1st October 1868, the Midland booking office at King's Cross was closed and the clerks were transferred to the new terminus across the road. One of the bodies opposing the Midland's Bill was the GNR, as the company would not only lose its annual £1,500, but the new line included rival stations in areas which it already served.

As previously mentioned, services between the GNR and the Metropolitan Railway had run since 1863, but again the additional traffic led to overcrowding of the existing tracks. Therefore the Metropolitan decided to double its capacity by adding the 'Widened Lines' which were brought into use between 1866 and 1868. The 'Widened Lines' commenced near the Metropolitan station at King's Cross, then continued to Moorgate Street. The route included a feature north of Farringdon Street which became known as the 'Ray Street Gridiron' and allowed the 'Widened Lines' to dive beneath the existing tracks so that they could surface on the opposite side of the formation.

Developments south of the Thames had resulted in connections between the Metropolitan and the London Chatham & Dover Railway, by way of a largely subterranean link through Snow Hill. The GNR supplied some of the finance for this venture and in return were granted running powers through to Herne Hill and Victoria. A passenger service linking King's Cross with

Ludgate Hill commenced operation on 20th February 1866, whilst a few months later, on 1st August, some of these workings were extended northwards to Hatfield and southwards to Herne Hill. The service, which ran on weekdays, comprised fifteen southbound trains and fourteen travelling in the opposite direction. GNR workings via the Metropolitan were suspended from 1st July 1867 until 1st March 1868 whilst the 'Widened Lines' were under construction, and when they resumed the Herne Hill trains were generally re-routed to Victoria.

A connection between the LCDR and the South Eastern Railway south of Blackfriars Bridge permitted the GNR to introduce a passenger service linking Finsbury Park and Woolwich from 1st June 1878. Originally there were six trains in each direction, but the number was subsequently increased to nine, with some continuing beyond Finsbury Park to either Enfield or Muswell Hill. They were apparently successful in their day, although inter-company squabbling between the LCDR and SER resulted in South Eastern passengers not being allowed to alight at 'Chatham' stations or vice versa.

As the years progressed the travelling habits of Londoners began to change, particularly after the advent of electric tramcars and tube railways. In many places the passenger receipts tumbled and some of the cross-town links faced an uncertain future. The service connecting the GNR with Woolwich ceased at the end of April 1907 with the Victoria trains following five months later.

Passengers wishing to save money in fares could travel on workmen's services, which all companies were obliged to provide after the Cheap Trains Act was passed in 1883. The GNR had actually been operating such trains from 1st March 1871, but at first the facility was only available on the 5.25am departure from Finsbury Park to Moorgate Street. The return fare of 2d offered a noticeable saving when compared to the standard cost and although the outward journey had to be made by one specified train, passengers could return at any time after the 5.51pm departure from Moorgate Street.

A further development, the Late Workmen's Ticket, allowed for greater flexibility and could be used on any services which reached their destination before 8am. These were valid from the majority of GNR suburban stations, including those on the main line between Hadley Wood and London. The return arrangements were even more attractive, as passengers could board any train after midday, although the savings were not as great as with ordinary workmen's tickets.

In addition to these facilities the company continued to operate a number of early morning trains specifically for workmen, including three which started from New Barnet in 1892 at 5.00am, 5.15am and 5.44am.

Workmen's tickets were understandably popular, but their title began to sound rather old fashioned so from 1st October 1950 the facility was replaced by Early Morning Returns.

This decade brought other, more notable changes, particularly with regard to train services, following the introduction of diesel working.

The first diesel multiple units were transferred to the King's Cross area in the autumn of 1958 and soon commenced operation. Each two-car unit could seat 115 passengers and they soon proved more economical to operate, particularly in the off-peak periods. Under the new regime there was a half-hourly service linking King's Cross with Hertford North and Hatfield, with one of the latter trains being extended to Welwyn Garden City. The journey time to Hatfield was only reduced by around three or four minutes, but BR management deemed the change to be beneficial.

For a number of years the majority of suburban services were worked by diesel multiple units, although they were supplemented in peak periods by loco-hauled trains formed of non-corridor stock.

Electrification in 1976-8 was the next logical step and many of today's commuters would find it impossible to imagine what it was like travelling on the trains which served their stations around fifty years ago. The old Great Northern & City, so long a Cinderella route, now has a frequent service of electric trains to and from the northern suburbs, whilst King's Cross continues to serve the East Coast Main Line as it has always done.

KING'S CROSS

1.   Here we see King's Cross station shortly after its opening on 14th October 1852. Lewis Cubitt's frontage was 300ft wide, of which the central portion accounted for 216ft; each trainshed roof being 105ft wide and 800ft long. King's Cross is the least altered of the early London termini, and the only subsequent change of note to the main buildings was the addition of offices above the cab road arcade on the east side in 1893. (Contemporary engraving, J.E. Connor collection)

2. We now come to a view looking east towards Pentonville Road with a goodly collection of horse drawn carts, hansom cabs, and buses. Until the early 1870s, St Pancras Road curved round alongside the GN Hotel and ran only a few yards in front of the King's Cross station frontage to join the other roads at the same point as Maiden Lane (York Way). After it was diverted, the enlarged King's Cross station forecourt accumulated an ever-changing collection of sheds and shops. This photograph was taken in 1899. A full-length iron 'porte cochere' canopy across the station frontage had been added around 1890 and lasted until the 1960s. The forecourt area was largely cleared for construction of the Victoria Line, followed by the erection of the present concourse building which opened in 1973. (The Gresley Society)

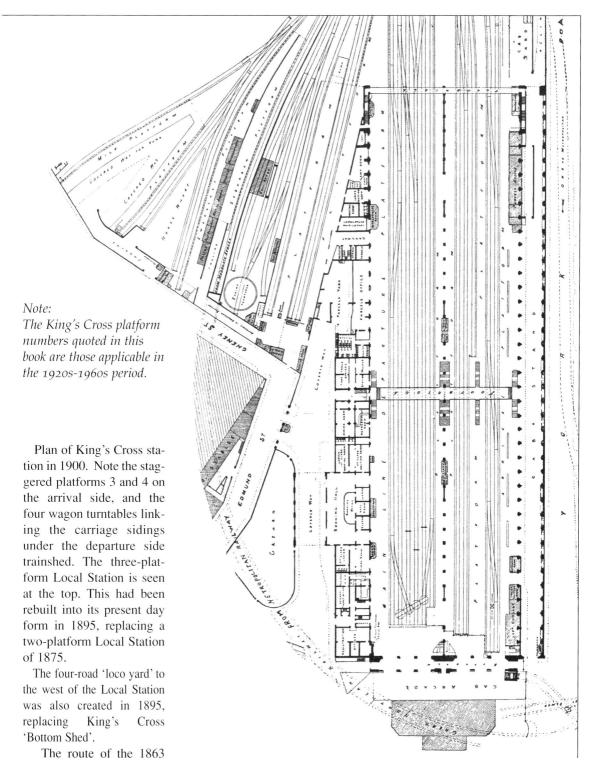

Note:
The King's Cross platform
numbers quoted in this
book are those applicable in
the 1920s-1960s period.

Plan of King's Cross station in 1900. Note the staggered platforms 3 and 4 on the arrival side, and the four wagon turntables linking the carriage sidings under the departure side trainshed. The three-platform Local Station is seen at the top. This had been rebuilt into its present day form in 1895, replacing a two-platform Local Station of 1875.

The four-road 'loco yard' to the west of the Local Station was also created in 1895, replacing King's Cross 'Bottom Shed'.

The route of the 1863 'Hotel Curve' is shown curving round beneath the frontage of the main line station. Until 1878 there was no platform on this curve, trains off the Met having to reverse into the main line departure platform. Platform 16 as we remember it was a reconstruction of 1895, when the line north of the tunnel mouth from the Met was moved further west to fit in the loco yard.

The horse and milk docks were also of 1895.

3. Moving inside the station, we see a train standing at platform 1 under the eastern 'arrival side' train shed in the 1900s. No. 1 had been the only arrival platform in the early years and its sole passenger amenities were the few rooms seen here. At left are platforms 2 and 3/4, opened in 1862: 3 (north end) and 4 (south end) were stepped as shown in the plan on the previous page, remaining so until 1934 when 3 was abolished and 4 lengthened. The footbridge across the platforms was provided in 1893 to link the main offices on the west side with the new office block over the cab road, but was also available for passenger use. It was removed at the end of 2008. (J.E. Connor collection)

4. In contrast, this late GNR period view of the western 'departure side' train shed is from the north end of the roof looking south. Platform 10 at right, originally the only departure platform, had almost all the station's passenger facilities behind it including the booking hall. The track layout here is as per the plan on the previous page, with four intermediate carriage sidings, then the island platform 6 (departure) and 5 (arrival) added in 1893 either side of the central arcade. Platforms 7 and 8 were not added until 1926. (Real Photographs)

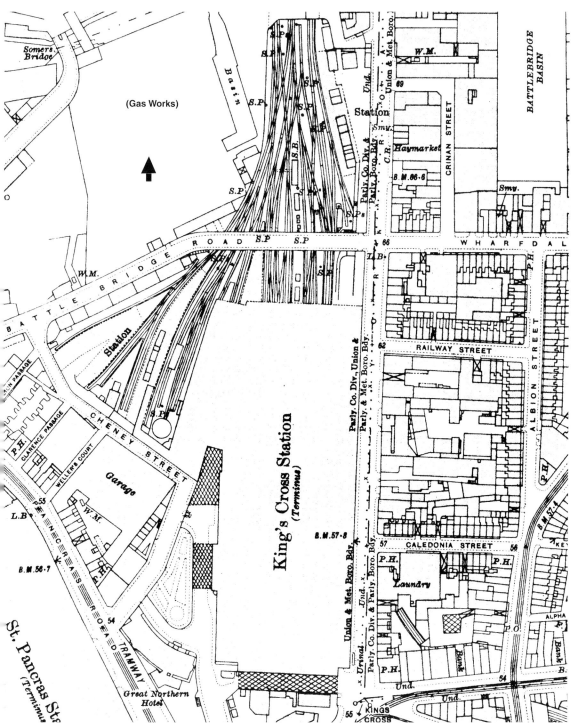

The 1913 OS map shows the station in its setting. the layout here is the same as in the 1900 plan. The area north of Cheney Street had been occupied by several streets of terraced housing up to the 1870s. Battle Bridge Road was constructed around 1890. Until 1912 there was a second road bridge, Congreve Street, over the station throat area, joining the Gas Works to York Way. The two bridges seriously obstructed the views from the signal boxes. The Gas Works canal basin was removed to make way for the 1923 loco yard (see picture 14).

5.   West of the station, between the frontage and St Pancras Road, stood the Great Northern Hotel, which is seen here. Also designed by Lewis Cubitt, the hotel welcomed its first guests in 1854 and featured a curved facade echoing the old alignment of St Pancras Road. The garden in the foreground lasted until LNER days, when it was replaced by a post office building. To the extreme left we see the clocktower of St. Pancras station, which is featured in the Middleton Press album *St. Pancras to St. Albans*. (The Gresley Society)

6.   Standing with our backs to the Great Northern Hotel, we see the main office block on the west side, which served as the headquarters of the GNR. A section of this was destroyed by enemy action in 1941, and has never been replaced. To the left of the picture is the entrance to the Local Station. The canopy between the two was added in 1900 to protect parcels traffic. (P. Kay)

7.   A sunny morning in the LNER period sees two N2 hauled trains ready to depart from platforms 12 and 14. None of the west side platforms could be used for arrivals until 1922, when the Up Carriage line through the middle tunnel was re-signalled to become the Up Relief. To the right can be seen platform 16, which was situated on the gradient up from the Metropolitan Widened Lines. (J.E. Connor collection)

8.   The overall roof of the Local Station dates from 1895/6. In this scene from the 1960s we are looking along platform 11, with the island platforms 12 and 13 on the left. The offices on the right filled the gap left after the first engine shed was demolished. The track in platform 13, here occupied by a van train, was lifted in the 1970s, but was reinstated in 1989 and is now known as platform 11. (Lens of Sutton collection)

9.   This view shows the arrangement immediately west of the Local Station trainshed, before platforms 14 and 15 were added in the 1920s. The locomotive yard here was needed to service locos between trips as there was neither time nor line capacity for them to go out to 'Top Shed'. The photographer is standing at the north end of platforms 16/17. (J.E. Connor collection)

10.   4-4-2T No. 1546, with condensing gear fitted for working over the Widened Lines, stands in the loco yard. The wall on the left is the back of the Local Station, while just visible to the right is the small coaling stage which is seen in the centre of the previous picture. (The Gresley Society)

11.   A later view from the north end of platforms 16/17, with the gradient up from the Metropolitan via the 'Hotel curve' very apparent. Above and to the left we can see the new 400ft island platform, comprising faces 14 and 15, which opened in 1924 on the site of the loco yard. This was needed as a greater proportion of suburban trains were starting from King's Cross instead of Moorgate. To the right of the post is platform 17, which was added along with 16 in 1895. This was the most remote part of the station to be penetrated by passengers, whilst the dock platforms, latterly used as a Motorail terminal, are located on the far right. (I. Baker)

12. Platforms 14 and 15 had their own concourse, from which we see a Brush Type 2 diesel loco- motive standing at the bufferstops on the left. These A1A-A1A diesels, which were later known as 'Class 31', served the line well and were regular performers on loco hauled suburban services until the 1970s. To the right stands the western wall of the Local Station's trainshed, whilst the departure indicator in the foreground advises passengers that only 2nd class accommodation was available on the trains. (Lens of Sutton collection)

13. This is platform 16, looking up hill during the early 1970s. In steam days passengers waiting here were choked by the frequent passing of down goods trains from the Southern Region. Only a few peak passenger trains ran in the last years but even with Class 31s there was still plenty of atmosphere. (G.L. Pring / Railway Record of the British Isles)

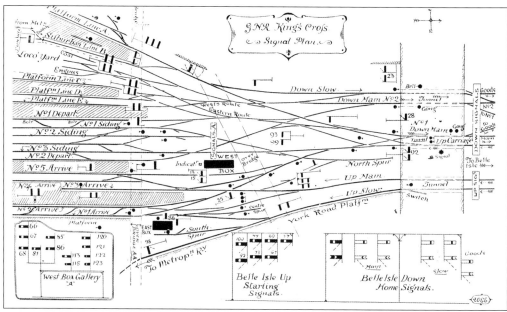

Signalling diagram of King's Cross, showing the station in 1905. The West and East signal boxes both dated from 1879. At this date the Local Station platforms were 'numbered' E, D and C, and platforms 16/17 were B and A. (The Railway Magazine)

14. This view from the 1950s shows the new locomotive yard which opened in 1923/4 to replace the facilities seen in pictures 9 and 10, lost to the construction of platforms 14 and 15. It was situated to the west of the existing lines, immediately south of Gasworks tunnel. The land had been purchased from the gas company, and required massive excavations and road realignment. The Battle Bridge Road overbridge was removed. The station throat area, which had previously been so hemmed in as to be almost un-photographable, was thus opened out to a format which is still recognisable today. The photographer is standing on the new Goods Way, which was constructed above the tunnel to replace Battle Bridge Road. (N.Simmons)

15. Here we can admire Class A1 Pacific No.1475 (later named *Flying Fox*) standing on the new 70ft LNER turntable in the 1920s. The 1923/4 retaining wall which supported the photographer of the previous view is seen behind. Further land above the retaining wall had been purchased by the railway for use as a motor vehicle depot. (J.E. Connor collection)

16.   This is the new power frame signal box of 1932, seen from platform 10. It became more familiar to us in its 1940 bricked-up state as seen in photo 20. It was built immediately south of the old West Box – indeed its north end could not be built until the old box was removed, hence its cleaner appearance than the rest of the boarding. The overhead routes for the signal cables had gone by the 1950s. At bottom right is the end of the new 1926 platforms 7/8, originally only 12ft wide but widened in 1938 when the remaining carriage siding was taken out. (RAS Marketing)

17.   Here we have a classic King's Cross departure, with the ever-present crowd of enthusiasts at the end of platform 10, as the first Peppercorn Class A1 Pacific No. 60114 *W.P. Allen* sets off with an express to the north. The covered footbridge along the north end of the trainshed roof rather spoilt its appearance from the 1890s to the 1960s. (Lens of Sutton collection)

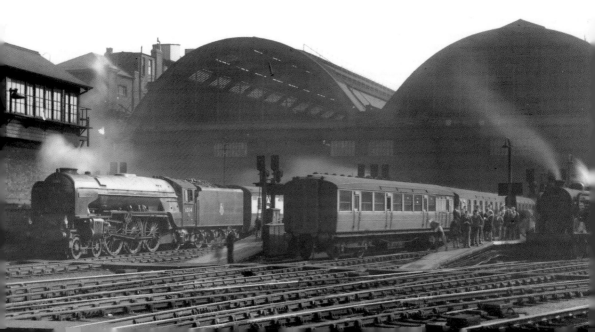

18.   On the east side of the station throat stood King's Cross York Road served by up trains heading for the Met Widened Lines. The original 1866 platform had to be demolished when the second (eastern) Gasworks tunnel was built, and this replacement platform 'two tracks further east' opened in March 1878. No alteration to the Met curve tunnel was needed. J52 No. 3922 is seen passing with an up goods, probably in the 1930s. (RAS Marketing)

19.   In this early 1970s view we can see the York Road canopy had been cut back, and the decorative valancing removed. The Class 31 is on a train to Moorgate. York Road platform closed on 8th November 1976 when the through service onto the Widened Lines was withdrawn, but it was temporarily re-opened for some terminating trains from 31st January 1977, before finally closing on the 5th March the same year. The new power box is glimpsed at top right. (J.E. Connor)

20.   No. 47409 arrives with an up train in platform 10 on 2nd October 1975, whilst Class 55 and Class 47 locomotives rest in the stabling sidings to the left. Although the 1932 signal box was still standing at the time, the signals had been worked by a temporary panel in the new power box since 1971. (T. Heavyside)

21.   The Class 55 'Deltics' were regarded by many as worthy successors to Sir Nigel Gresley's Pacifics on East Coast main line services, with some continuing the tradition of being named after famous racehorses and others commemorating regiments. Here we see No. 55013 *The Black Watch* awaiting departure with the 20.00 to Aberdeen on a wet 6th July 1980. (T. Heavyside)

22. In spring 1977 the whole station throat area was relaid to a new simpler layout, with the eastern Gasworks tunnel being abandoned. Electrification and resignalling were implemented at the same time. Here the up 'Bradford Executive' is seen arriving on 23rd August 1988. (T. Heavyside)

London, Highgate, High Barnet.	161	Edgware, Hatfield, and Hitchin.

LONDON, HIGHGATE, HIGH BARNET, EDGWARE, HATFIELD, & HITCHIN.—Great Northern.

Week Days—Continued below.

Extract from the 1890 Great Northern Railway's suburban timetable.

23. Outside the station, to the north of the local platforms and the former Motorail terminal, stood Culross Buildings, named after the chairman of the GNR. They were erected in 1891 on the south side of Battle Bridge Road and housed railway staff. This picture dates from the late 1990s. (P. Kay).

KING'S CROSS
GOODS YARD

HER MAJESTY'S DEPARTURE FROM THE GREAT NORTHERN RAILWAY TERMINUS, AT KING'S-CROSS.

24.   The oldest buildings in what became King's Cross Goods Yard started life as the original London passenger terminus of the GNR. Although only a temporary measure, it sported an impressive overall roof, supported on cast iron columns, linked by cast spandrel beams. It opened on 7th August 1850, and closed with the opening of the new King's Cross station on 14th October 1852. The station, known as 'King's Cross' whilst in use but generally referred to as 'Maiden Lane' in the construction period, is known only from this one sketch of August 1851, depicting the royal family entering their train en route to Scotland. The artist is positioned at the south end of the eastern span of Lewis Cubitt's twin-span trainshed roof. Note the North London train in the background. In 1852 this area became a Potato Market, with a major reconstruction in 1864 to improve the facilities. However the 1850 roofs survived until c1970, ignored by all. The main station building (behind the artist here) was demolished in 1864 and no views of it are known. (Illustrated London News)

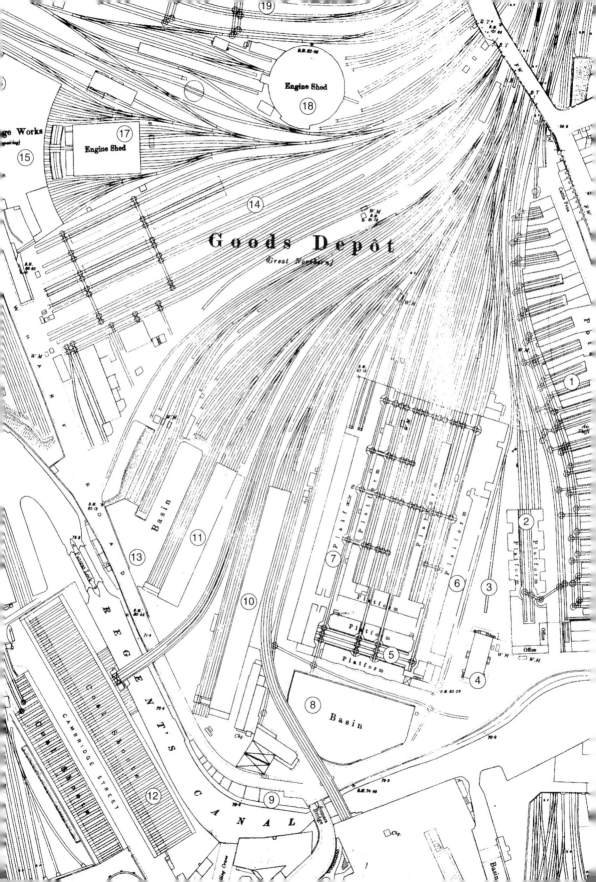

Goods Depôt
(Great Northern)

Engine Shed
(18)

(19)

Engine Shed
(17)

ge Works
(15)

(14)

(13)

(11)

Basin

(10)

(7)

(6)

(3)

(2)

(1)

(5)

(4)

(8) Basin

REGENT'S CANAL

CAMBRIDGE STREET

(12)

(9)

25. The six-storey Granary block was Lewis Cubitt's most impressive piece of work amongst the Kings Cross Goods Yard buildings. It was 180ft by 100ft in plan, and 70ft high. Unusually for the period, this 1853 illustration slightly underplays the height. It survives today without external alteration. To the left is the single-storey Departure Goods Shed, with the similar Arrival Goods Shed to the right. Canal boats had access to the Granary and both the Goods Sheds. The canal transfer facility was provided principally for access to shipping, and lost importance once rail links were provided to the docks, leading to the basin being filled in. The GNR commenced goods traffic here in November 1850. After rail traffic ended the Granary and the 1850 Goods Sheds became an NCL depot.

The 1894 Ordnance Survey map opposite shows the following:
1   Potato Warehouses (1864) underneath 1850 passenger station roofs.
2   1850 Carriage Shed, became Midland Railway Goods Shed, subsequently used for
     warehousing by GNR and referred to as the 'Midland Shed'.
3   1888 roofing either side of the 'Midland Shed'.
4   1850 Goods Offices block.
5   Granary (1850/1).
6   1850 Goods Shed (Arrival Shed).
7   1850 Goods Shed (Departure Shed).
8   Canal Basin for general goods traffic transfer (1850).
9   Fish & Coal Offices block.
10 GNR Eastern Coal Drops (1851).
11 GNR Western Coal Drops (1860). [Incorporated into Western Goods Shed 1899].
12 Samuel Plimsoll's Coal Drops (1866).
13 Canal Basin for coal and stone traffics transfer (1850). [Western Goods Shed built on site 1899].
14 1850s sidings.
15 1850 Engine Shed, later 'Erecting Shop'.
16 1862 extension for Carriage & Wagon Shops. [Became 'Met Shed' 1932].
17 1862 Engine Shed ('Main Line Running Shed').
18 Midland Roundhouse (1859), later used by GNR as running shed for tank locos until demolished 1931.
19 Coal Depot sidings 1863/4 .

26.   The 'Potato Warehouses' built in 1864 underneath the passenger station roofs comprised a 900ft row of 36 small 'warehouses' each fronted by an office. Rail traffic ceased in the 1960s but many of the potato dealers remained in occupation, with road delivery. By the time of this 1982 photograph (looking down from York Way) all that remained was the office sections of Nos 4 to 23, and these too were demolished in 1988-90. (P. Kay)

27.   The GNR's Potato Market was so successful that it overflowed into the open areas either side of the 'Midland Shed'. The GNR was long indifferent to the potato men's complaints of being rained on, but was spurred into action in 1888 when the Midland tried to lure the dealers away to Somers Town! This resulted in the area on both sides of the Midland Shed being covered over with the 'Handyside roofs' (as they are now called). This is the 52ft-wide 1888 roof between the Midland Shed (left) and the now-demolished 1850 pas-senger station roofs (right). The cast-iron spandrel beams in the 18-arch arcade seen here date from 1850, and they are now the sole remaining portion of the passenger station roof. The two brick 'chimneys' at right in this 1996 view are air shafts for the second Gasworks Tunnel bore of 1878. (P. Kay)

28. The original Coal Drops of 1851, known as the Eastern Coal Drops after 1860, are seen here in 1996 after several of the Goods Yard buildings had been let off to a multiplicity of small tenants, providing free public access to this formerly secret world. The rail tracks were at upper level; bulk storage of coal at middle level; and 'bagging-up' cells with road vehicle access at road level. In later GNR days most of this building was used for general goods warehousing. (P. Kay)

29. The west wall of the 1899 Western Goods Shed, seen from the far side of the Regents Canal. The bricked-up entrance to the former Coal & Stone canal basin is conspicuous. Always the least 'appreciated' of the Goods Yard buildings, the Western Goods Shed is to be demolished in the forthcoming redevelopment of the site; all the other surviving buildings will be retained. (P. Kay)

30.   In this wonderful view from the top of the new LNER loco coaling tower, we can see the Western Goods Shed on the left. This view typifies railway goods yards before the rise of road haulage took away so much traffic, and containerisation on the railways led to the old fashioned 'goods yard' being replaced by the 'container terminal'. The Midland line is seen in the background. (The Gresley Society)

31.   The full length of the office block on the north side of the Western Goods Shed is better appreciated in this 1990s view. (P. Kay)

32.   What can one say of the far-famed 'Top Shed' in an album of this size? This late 1930s view of the Main Line Running Shed captures everything that the place meant. The main structure of the shed was never altered, but a new flat roof had to be provided in 1949 after war damage to the original. Top Shed closed entirely in June 1963. (The Gresley Society)

33.   Far more humdrum was the 'Met Shed', a make-do of 1932 to house the depot's tank engines after the demolition of the Midland Roundhouse. The front half of it was part of the original 1850 running shed, the rear half dated from 1862 when the 1850 running shed buildings were extended to serve as carriage & wagon shops. (The Gresley Society)

34.   This is a pre-grouping era view of the Midland Roundhouse (sometimes called the 'Derby Shed'). It was built by the GNR for the Midland Railway's use and opened in February 1859. The Midland vacated it in 1868, after which it became a carriage & wagon shop for a while, and then a running shed for the GNR's tank locos. It was demolished in 1931; the lines were used for open-air stabling until the Met Shed opened. (J.E. Connor collection)

35.   Venturing inside the Midland Roundhouse in the late GNR period, we find C2 Class 4-4-2T No.1506, J6 0-6-0 No.101, and F2 0-4-2 No.112. Sunlight slants in through the arched windows to cast a brilliant glow across 1506's cab and tank sides, and casts highlights on her shed-mates. 1506 is still carrying condensing gear, but a comparison with the picture of her classmate at King's Cross in picture no. 10 shows this version of the apparatus to be rather less obtrusive. (J.E. Connor Collection)

BELLE ISLE

This is how Belle Isle appeared on the 1913 OS map. In the early years there was just a simple double-track junction, north of the NLR viaduct, between the lines to the Goods Yard and the lines to King's Cross. This was 'Copenhagen Junction'. The 'Belle Isle' name did not appear in GNR usage until 1869; it was the rather ironic name of an area of noxious industries on the west side of the railway. Subsequent developments here were dictated principally by the opening of the second and third bores of the Gasworks and Copenhagen Tunnels, each of which required significant track alterations. In both cases the middle tunnel was the original. The order of change was as follows:

1877 – second (western) Copenhagen Tunnel, for Up and Down Goods lines. In connection with the viaduct at the north end of the tunnel this separated out goods and passenger trains at Holloway with non-conflicting moves.

1878 - second (eastern) Gasworks Tunnel, carrying the Up Fast and Up Slow. With this the general ambience of Belle Isle reached the form that lasted until the 1970s.

1886 - third (eastern) Copenhagen Tunnel, carrying the Up Fast and Up Slow (the original tunnel now taking the Down Slow and Down Fast).

1892 – third (western) Gasworks Tunnel. This was a difficult job as it passed only a few feet below the 'Midland Shed' and the Potato Market buildings. (The original Gasworks Tunnel had been built cut-and-cover before any of the buildings above were started on).

A conspicuous feature of the upper part of this extract is the line built 1877/8 to serve the GNR's new Caledonian Road Goods Depot (1878-1967). This rose on viaduct behind Goods & Mineral Junction signal box, up to a reversing spur in a cutting directly above the Copenhagen tunnels. The Goods Depot itself is off map to the right.

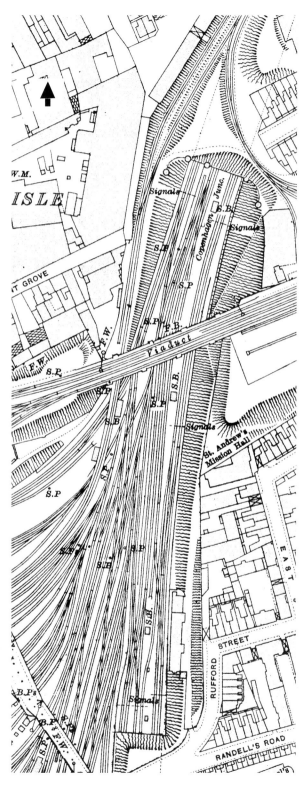

36. This view shows the pointwork and signals at the entrance to the Goods Yard. The signal box to the left was called Five Arch Bridge. It was an 1899 reconstruction of an older box, whose name derived from the fact that the York Way viaduct originally only consisted of the five arches seen here. The bridge was extended northwards in 1863/4 to span the new coal yard sidings. Most of the signals at this box were left 'normally off', allowing shunt moves from the Goods Yard; they were only put to danger when an up arrival was approaching.
(G.L. Pring / Railway Record of the British Isles)

37. Here we have an unusual view of Goods & Mineral Junction signal box looking south from under the western span of the NLR viaduct. The passenger lines are out of view to the left. The line passing under the bridge to the right is the curve which met the North London Railway at St Pancras Junction box. This was opened in 1862 and singled in the early BR years. The bridge carried the line up to Caledonian Road goods depot, which was accessed via a headshunt ending at Blundell Street. Goods & Mineral Junction box opened in 1877 and soldiered on (along with Five Arch Bridge) until September 1975.
(G.L. Pring / Railway Record of the British Isles)

38.   Belle Isle is seen here in all its glory, as Atlantic No.1460 heads for Holloway with a down Pullman, whilst Great Central 4-6-0 No.1167 waits on the Up South London Goods line which also formed the route for locos from Top Shed to Kings Cross. Belle Isle Down signal box is glimpsed at left; it was closed in 1935. In the background the endless shunt moves from the Goods Yard are being played out. (The Gresley Society)

39.   The Great Northern Cemetery Company's Kings Cross Funeral Station was an expensive failure, being used for its intended purpose only from 1861 to 1863. In 1875 the company sold it to the GNR who needed to widen the line here in connection with the second Gasworks Tunnel. The 'trainshed' along the west side of the building was removed for the widening, however the rest of the building continued to brood over the lines below until 1962. It features as backdrop in many photographs, such as this view of 60062 *Minoru* from the 1950s. (The Gresley Society)

40.   In this 1900s view we are looking north towards the Copenhagen Tunnels. C2 class 4-4-2T No.1524, built in 1901, drifts out of the eastern bore on the Up Fast with a suburban working. A great defect of the pre-1970s Kings Cross layout was that all up trains for the 'Suburban station' had to run on the Up Fast from Holloway and then cross over the entire station throat layout, blocking departure moves. The three tunnel mouths here were made a harmonious composition despite their different levels and dates. (F. Moore's Railway Photographs)

41.   Belle Isle Up box was opened in 1886 in connection with the third Copenhagen Tunnel, and lasted until 1968. Here we see No. 60125 arriving with an up express in the 1950s, whilst No. 60032 waits light engine on the South London Siding (as it had become known by this date) waiting for a path down into the terminus. (D.I.D. Loveday / The Gresley Society)

42. This view is taken from a spot above the south portals of Copenhagen tunnel; a few intrepid photographers made their way through the Caledonian Road Goods Yard, which had its entrance in Frederick Street, to reach this point directly above the down lines. The vista was made famous in the early 1950s when it served as the backdrop to the Ealing Comedy, *The Ladykillers*, in which a gang of robbers meet their doom here in various sticky ways. The 1874-1967 Copenhagen Junction signal box is seen at bottom left. Trains are passing on the Up Fast and Down Slow. The layout here enabled goods trains from the Southern Region to the Goods Yard to reverse inside the tunnel, and vice versa. The Great Northern and North London Railways were planned at the same time as each other in the late 1840s, and the earliest engravings of the approaches to King's Cross feature the North London viaduct spanning the cutting. The North London Railway's Maiden Lane station, closed in 1917, was situated about 200 yards to the west of this view. (D.I.D. Loveday / The Gresley Society)

HOLLOWAY

43. In the early 1970s one could look out from the north end of Copenhagen Tunnel over a scene unchanged since the 1880s. The lines at the tunnel mouths here are (from left) Down Goods / Up Goods, Down Slow / Down Fast, and Up Fast / Up Slow. The 1877 Up Goods viaduct was lengthened at its north end in 1886 to fit in the new up lines beneath. In 1976/7 large scale works were undertaken here to provide a new viaduct for the Up Slow line, so that up suburban trains could reach the west side 'suburban' platforms at Kings Cross without blocking down departures. The lines through the western tunnel then became Down Slow/Up Slow, those through the original tunnel Up Fast/Up Slow, and the eastern bore was abandoned. (G.L. Pring / Railway Record of the British Isles)

44. After Holloway station closed, some photographers adopted the up side of the line by Caledonian Road bridge as a vantage point. In this 1920s scene Gresley Class A1 4-6-2 No. 2545 *Diamond Jubilee* on the 9.50am from Kings Cross is passing a down goods train. The signals on the left are Belle Isle Up's outer distants. The cutting slope on the down side provided a large area for staff allotments. (The Gresley Society)

45. A generation later, and nothing has changed save for replacement upper quadrant signal arms. On a sunny 17th June 1955 N2 0-6-2T No. 69586 heads a morning down train formed of the BR suburban stock that later provided atmospheric watercolour-filled journeys for Class 31-hauled 1970s commuters. The tasteful shrubs planted by the LNER were an unusual adornment in the British railway scene. (P.H. Groom)

46. The 1 in 110 gradient shows clearly as Thompson Class L1 2-6-4T No. 67779 passes Caledonian Road overbridge and the 1900-1976 Holloway South Down box with a down ECS working on 31st August 1961. The photographer is standing on the cattle platform by Holloway South Up box. (P.H. Groom)

47. This would be the Second Man's view of the gradient from a train on the Down Slow in 1973. The nearest group of up signals dated from 1900 and had been at the south end of Holloway station up platform (see picture 49). The coaching stock directly ahead is in Holloway Carriage Sidings. Holloway North Down box is seen in the distance. (A.A. Jackson)

Holloway station started as a Ticket Platform for up trains. From 1852 passengers were allowed to alight here, and a down platform was added in about 1856, after which it functioned as a normal station. The wide up island platform seen here was built in 1865/6; the down island platform was a replacement of 1900/1. The station entrance building (of which no photographs have been traced) was on the southwest side of Holloway Road at street level, between the main line bridges and the separate two-track bridge for the 1894 Down Goods / Down Carriage lines. Holloway Cattle Depot (bottom) opened in 1854, ready for the opening of the nearby New Metropolitan Cattle Market in 1855. The layout seen here dated from the 1880s. Cattle traffic ceased in the 1930s, and the platforms became a Motorail terminal in the 1960s. The down side Carriage Sidings opened in 1865, were much enlarged in 1893, and closed in the 1970s. The 'Station' shown in Holloway Road to the east of the main line is the GNP&B's Holloway Road station, which along with Caledonian Road abstracted so much of the GNR's traffic that Holloway station was closed for good on 1st October 1915, only a year after the Ordnance Survey published this revision. By 1921 the platforms had been removed.

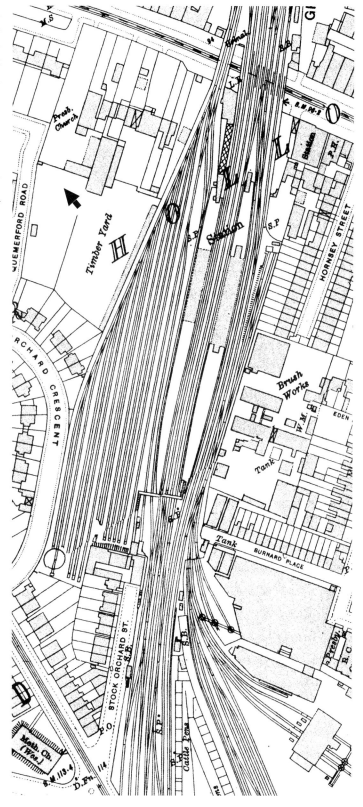

48.   Holloway station was a favourite spot for train photographers in the 1895-1915 period. They focused on down expresses, where the locos were working hard, but nobody seems to have photographed the station buildings properly! This view must date from 1899/1900 as it shows the early stages of work for the new down platform. The signal box glimpsed on the left is Holloway South (alias Holloway Station Down), opened in 1876 and replaced by South Down in 1900. The footbridge in the background formed the access route from a second station entrance in Stock Orchard Street. The famed Ivatt Small Atlantic No. 990 *Henry Oakley* heading this down express was new in 1898. (J.E. Connor collection)

49.   This photograph must have been taken in 1901/2 as the brickwork of the new down platform of 1900/1 is still in pristine state. The 'Holloway & Caledonian Road' name was adopted from 6th May 1901. At Holloway after 1901 there were four tracks between the platforms, as the new island down platform was served by the Down Slow No.2 on the east side and the Down Goods on the west side. Here there is an ECS train on the Down Goods, and behind it the roofs of other stock in the Carriage Sidings. Stirling Single No. 666, seen working this express, was withdrawn in 1906. (J.E. Connor collection)

50.   Finally we see large Atlantic No. 299 pass through. The new down platform buildings are only known from glimpses like this. The large timber-built block on the up platform was erected in 1866; it had been ordered for Wood Green but was diverted here after indecision on the works at the latter station. No. 299 was built at Doncaster Works in 1905 and was withdrawn for scrapping in May 1945. (J.E. Connor collection)

51.   In this view of Holloway North Up box, we are looking towards Kings Cross. Holloway North Up was the most remarkable of all the GNR signal boxes in London. The nearer gable-to-track section dated from 1867 and was probably the first interlocked box on the main line in London. The remainder of the box was an 1886 extension. The whole base was bricked up in 1940, as most boxes in London were. This photograph dates from 1970 and shows evidence of work in progress on the up side layout rationalisation which brought the abolition of the box on 26th July 1970. (The Gresley Society)

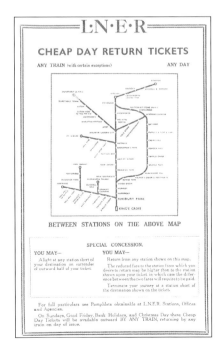

FINSBURY PARK

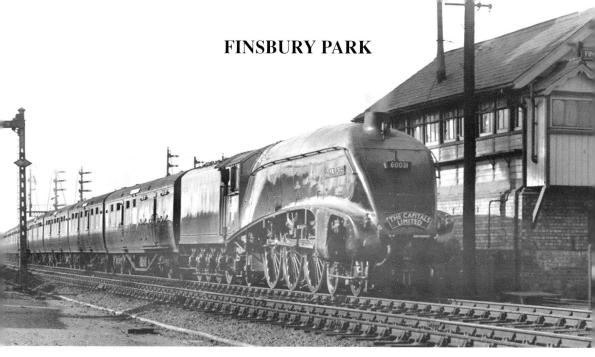

52.   Class A4 4-6-2 No. 60032 *Golden Plover* storms past Finsbury Park No.3 box with the down 'Capitals Limited' on 3rd September 1949. The somersault gantry behind lasted until 1955, latterly the last somersaults on the main line in London. (D.A. Dant / The Gresley Society)

53.   Beneath the Pacific-hauled expresses, there was a less-known Finsbury Park of goods yards and goods depots. This view was taken from Drayton Park LT box in July 1960. The coaching stock at left is in the siding which ran down to the GN&C carriage sheds. Beyond the BR van are the sidings to the GNR gas and electric works, and Ashburton Grove goods depot. Finsbury Park No.1 box in the foreground was one of the 1874 boxes. Ashburton Grove box is seen under the main line bridge, and East Goods box 'upstairs'. (A. A. Jackson)

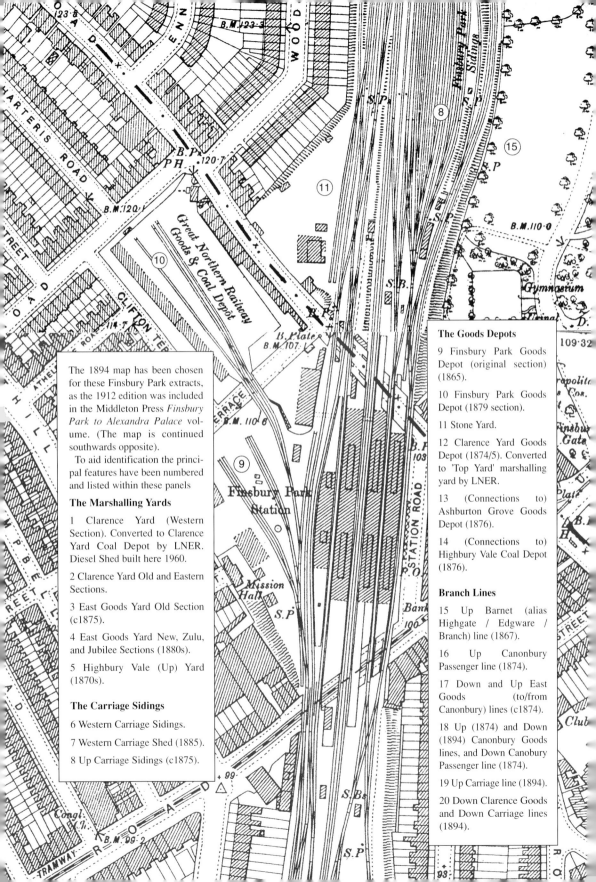

The 1894 map has been chosen for these Finsbury Park extracts, as the 1912 edition was included in the Middleton Press *Finsbury Park to Alexandra Palace* volume. (The map is continued southwards opposite).

To aid identification the principal features have been numbered and listed within these panels

The Marshalling Yards

1 Clarence Yard (Western Section). Converted to Clarence Yard Coal Depot by LNER. Diesel Shed built here 1960.

2 Clarence Yard Old and Eastern Sections.

3 East Goods Yard Old Section (c1875).

4 East Goods Yard New, Zulu, and Jubilee Sections (1880s).

5 Highbury Vale (Up) Yard (1870s).

The Carriage Sidings

6 Western Carriage Sidings.

7 Western Carriage Shed (1885).

8 Up Carriage Sidings (c1875).

The Goods Depots

9 Finsbury Park Goods Depot (original section) (1865).

10 Finsbury Park Goods Depot (1879 section).

11 Stone Yard.

12 Clarence Yard Goods Depot (1874/5). Converted to 'Top Yard' marshalling yard by LNER.

13 (Connections to) Ashburton Grove Goods Depot (1876).

14 (Connections to) Highbury Vale Coal Depot (1876).

Branch Lines

15 Up Barnet (alias Highgate / Edgware / Branch) line (1867).

16 Up Canonbury Passenger line (1874).

17 Down and Up East Goods (to/from Canonbury) lines (c1874).

18 Up (1874) and Down (1894) Canonbury Goods lines, and Down Canobury Passenger line (1874).

19 Up Carriage line (1894).

20 Down Clarence Goods and Down Carriage lines (1894).

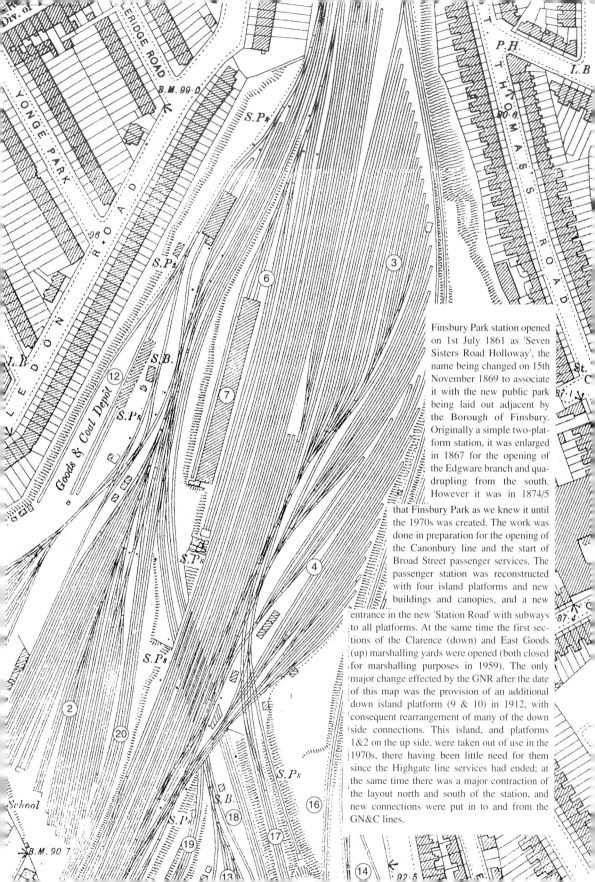

Finsbury Park station opened on 1st July 1861 as 'Seven Sisters Road Holloway', the name being changed on 15th November 1869 to associate it with the new public park being laid out adjacent by the Borough of Finsbury. Originally a simple two-platform station, it was enlarged in 1867 for the opening of the Edgware branch and quadrupling from the south. However it was in 1874/5 that Finsbury Park as we knew it until the 1970s was created. The work was done in preparation for the opening of the Canonbury line and the start of Broad Street passenger services. The passenger station was reconstructed with four island platforms and new buildings and canopies, and a new entrance in the new 'Station Road' with subways to all platforms. At the same time the first sections of the Clarence (down) and East Goods (up) marshalling yards were opened (both closed for marshalling purposes in 1959). The only major change effected by the GNR after the date of this map was the provision of an additional down island platform (9 & 10) in 1912, with consequent rearrangement of many of the down side connections. This island, and platforms 1&2 on the up side, were taken out of use in the 1970s, there having been little need for them since the Highgate line services had ended; at the same time there was a major contraction of the layout north and south of the station, and new connections were put in to and from the GN&C lines.

54.   Ex-Great Eastern Railway 'Royal Claud' 4-4-0 No. 8787 is seen at the Up Fast platform at an unknown date, in the 1930s. The fencing along the middle of this island was put in when the ticket checking for up expresses was transferred here from Holloway. (R.A.S. Marketing)

55.   A glimpse of the workaday railway as Class J14 0-6-0ST No.111 (built 1897) passes over the Seven Sisters Road bridges on the Down Goods. The connections to Finsbury Park Goods Depot are in the foreground. (J.E. Connor collection)

56. 'Vertically-stacked' signal arms lasted at Finsbury Park into BR days, long after this practice had in theory been ended on passenger lines. Here C12 4-4-2T No.7374 (1947 number) waits on the Down Slow No.2 line with an Alexandra Palace train in about 1950. No.5 box is half-seen in the distance. One's image of the line is distorted by the general absence from the photographic record of views taken on the all-too-common murky days such as this. (J. F. Aylard)

57. Here we see the down platforms in 1960. At far left is the 1912 additional island 10 and 9, serving the Down Canonbury and Down Slow No.2 lines; then 8 and 7 (1874) serving the Down Slow No.2 and Down Slow No.1; and at right 6 and 5 (1867/61) serving the Down Slow No.1 and Down Fast. The station was famed for the way in which, in the evening peak, two or three down trains from King's Cross, Moorgate, and Broad Street would arrive at the platforms together, and the passengers interchanging between them would rush through the compartments of the middle train instead of using the subways. (Stations UK)

58.   Finsbury Park with its elevated situation was always known as a windy place with horizontal rain, but became even more so after 1965 when all the platform canopies were removed (except those on 9 and 10, which lasted until this platform was taken out of use in 1973). The down platforms are seen here in this denuded form in the late 1960s. The remaining platforms received new, much shorter, canopies in the 1970s. Most of the yellow brick 1874 platform buildings were still in use in 2008. (J.E. Connor)

59. Peppercorn Class A1 4-6-2 No. 60163 passes admiring onlookers at Finsbury Park as she heads towards King's Cross on Saturday 7th February 2009 with *The Talisman* special train from Darlington. No. 60163 was built by the A1 Steam Locomotive Trust and made her main line passenger debut in January 2009. Initially she ran without nameplates but twelve days after this view was taken the locomotive was officially named *Tornado* by H.R.H. Prince Charles. This was her first run into London and the shadows to the left give some idea of the crowd which turned out to watch her pass. (J.E. Connor)

FINSBURY PARK DEPOT

60. Finsbury Park diesel depot opened in 1960. It symbolised the new age in which the GN line would be home to the country's fastest trains. All is green, clean, and modern in this early 1960s view. The depot was close to housing but it was innocently (and incorrectly) assumed that nobody would object to something so modern. (G.W. Goslin collection)

61. Like many projects of its time, the diesel depot was not to have a long life and closed in 1981. In this view, taken on the 8th May that year, 55015 and 47210 are passed by a new-order HST. To the left are the Down Moorgate, Down Canonbury, and Down Goods lines in their 1970s form. (T. Heavyside)

NORTH OF FINSBURY PARK

62.   The eponymous Park did not impinge much on the average passenger's perceptions of the station, however a vision of greenery could be gained by walking to the country end of the platforms. On this wet summer's day in 1962 Class A3 4-6-2 No. 60107 *Royal Lancer* is seen passing over the Stroud Green Road bridges on an up express, with Nos 5 and 6 boxes and the Up Carriage Sidings behind. (G. Silcock)

63.   Around the same time, Brush Type 2 A1A-A1A No. D5587 is captured from the window of No.6 box with an up suburban service formed of two quad-art sets. The up Barnet branch flyover is seen in the background. The down side lines were all at a higher level after 1888, in order to reduce the gradient on the viaduct for down branch trains. No.5 box was built in 1888 in connection with this work. (G. Silcock)

HARRINGAY

Harringay station was a late development, for as late as the 1870s there was
nothing but empty fields in the vicinity.
It was built under a guarantee from the
British Land Company who were
developing the area between Green
Lanes and Wightman Road, and opened
for passenger traffic on 1st May 1885,
and for goods around the same time.
The overhead booking office was situated off a footbridge linking Wightman
Road with Quernmore Road on the west
side, where separate housing developments were afoot. The 1885 station
buildings were never significantly
altered prior to the 1960s. The up island
platform served the Up Fast and Up
Slow. The down platform was originally single-sided serving the Down Slow,
but became an island in 1900 when the
former Down Goods running behind it
became a passenger line the Down
Slow No.2. The Tottenham &
Hampstead line is seen at bottom. The
rear fences of the gardens of the houses
in Stapleton Hall Road (bottom left)
betray the alignment of the Harringay
Curve, which had existed unused from
1867 to c1875, was relaid in 1916 but
again remained unused until lifted in
1920, and finally saw use after being
relaid again in 1940. The footpath along
the top of the cutting north of the station
afforded good views for the enthusiast
(picture 73). This hill, the 'Hog's Back',
was the eastern end of the Northern
Heights, and the cause of the GN line's
eastward track via Finsbury Park before
turning to the desired northwesterly
alignment. At the top of this extract are
the 1893 'viaduct lines' which provided
the only connection between the up and
down sides at Ferme Park, used for
light engine moves, wagon transfers,
and later for goods workings via the
Harringay Curve. The map shown dates
from 1894.

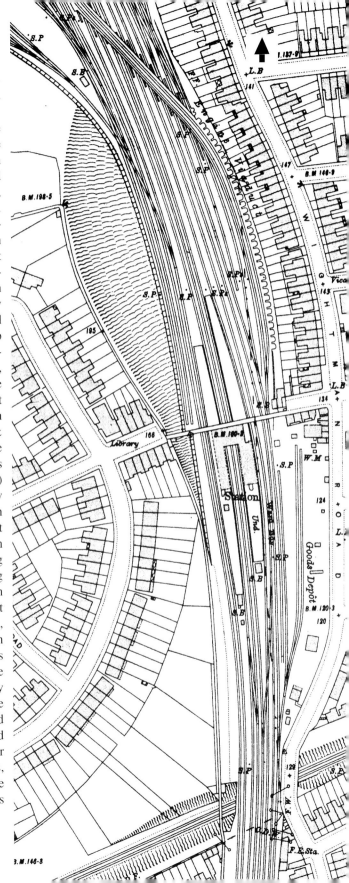

Great Northern Railway

"THE NORTHERN HEIGHTS."

London's Healthiest and Most Accessible Suburbs.

BRACING BARNET	HEALTHY SOUTHGATE	BREEZY HIGHGATE
Pastoral and Woodland Scenery.	Charming Countryside.	Pleasant Woodlands.
King's Cross–16 Min.	King's Cross–13 Min	King's Cross–13 Min.
SEASON TICKETS 6d. PER DAY.	SEASON TICKETS 4½d. PER DAY.	SEASON TICKETS 2½d. PER DAY.

PALMER'S GREEN AND WINCHMORE HILL	WOODSIDE PARK AND TOTTERIDGE	PICTURESQUE FINCHLEY
Enfield Chase and New River District.	Rural Surroundings and Pure Air	Attractive Villa Residences.
King's Cross–18 Min.		King's Cross–17 Min.
SEASON TICKETS 4½d. and 5d. PER DAY.	SEASON TICKETS 5½d. and 6d. PER DAY.	SEASON TICKETS 4½d. PER DAY.

EXCHANGE FOG FOR SUNSHINE	COUNTRY HOMES IN	1st, 2nd, 3rd CLASS SEASON TICKETS
Compare London's Rents and Taxes. with those	BEDFORDSHIRE AND	AT EXCEPTIONALLY
IN THE SUBURBS.	CAMBRIDGESHIRE.	LOW RATES.

Frequent Trains and Cheap Rates make it possible to combine

THE PLEASURES OF THE COUNTRY
:: WITH :: (Gardening, Tennis, Golf, etc.)

THE PRIVILEGES OF TOWN
(Theatres, Clubs, Shops and Schools.)

The Railway Company will give every assistance to those seeking Healthy Homes.

London ; King's Cross Station.   OLIVER BURY, *General Manager.*

64. For decades the North London tanks and their trains of four-wheelers on the Broad Street services were one of the principal features of the GN lines in London, but they were not photographed to the same extent as the Great Northern expresses. Here we see a down train calling at Harringay in the 1890s, with the down platform in its original form with a brick wall behind.
(J.E. Connor collection)

←

Advertisement extolling the joys of suburban living, taken from a 1908 GNR guide book entitled *Where To Live.*

65.   In this view, Class D2 4-4-0 No.1077 passes through Harringay on the Up Fast with a special working including a carriage truck. The hipped-roof timber-built booking office on girders over the tracks served as a model for those built later at Hornsey, New Southgate, and New Barnet, although there were detail variations. (J.E. Connor collection)

66.   This view from around 1930 shows the down platform in its post-1900 island form. The western end of the footbridge had also been rebuilt in 1900. Stirling 0-6-0 No.4138 (fitted with this domed boiler in 1927) has been given a run on the Down Fast with this engineers train. (J.E. Connor collection)

67. In this view we are looking south from Harringay down platform in 1938. The footpath on the west side of the line was a favourite place for boys to 'cop' locos in the 1930s, but there is an extra-large crowd here to see the special run of the restored GNR No.1, which can be seen approaching. The two lines to the west of the down platform (post-1900) were the Down Slow No.2 and Down Goods. The Harringay Down box seen here was the third of that name, opening in 1903. It took over the up side also in 1924 when Harringay Up (seen on the OS) was abolished, and closed in 1973. The bushes at right are on the alignment of the Harringay Curve. (Lens of Sutton collection)

68. After the T&H curve was reinstated in 1940, trains regularly ran through from Feltham to the GN this way. In this early 1960s view No. 33021, having arrived at Ferme Park down side via the curve with a special for Ferme Park Up Yard, has reversed back over the viaduct line. Harringay Up Goods box (1893-1974) was the tallest box on the GN in London, the signalman needing to see over the station footbridge. (D.I.D. Loveday / The Gresley Society)

69. Here we have a northward view taken around 1967. When the down platform became an island the buildings were left as before, with no canopy on the west side. The booking office building had suffered a fire in the mid-1960s and was left unrepaired, before being largely removed around 1968. The station had been renamed 'Harringay West' on 18th June 1951 (it reverted to 'Harringay' on 27th May 1971, although the ER nameboard seen here lasted for some time after that). In the 1960s the DMUs worked the off-peak services, with the loco-hauled sets supplementing in the Mon-Fri peaks. The Cravens units were based in Finsbury Park up sidings. (J.E. Connor)

70. The footbridge gave a good view northwards for those of sufficient height. It is July 1962 here, and traditional goods traffic is still flourishing. The diesel shunter is engaged in a shunt from Ferme Park Down Yard on one of the shunt spur lines. Beyond the signal gantry is the 1931-1969 Ferme Park South Down box, provided in connection with an LNER expansion of the Down Yard (and well to the south of its predecessor seen on the 1914 OS). Meanwhile a steam-hauled goods is passing on the Down Slow No.1. In the background are the replacement 1961 bridge spans for the Viaduct lines. (D.I.D. Loveday / The Gresley Society)

71. On bad days the whole Ferme Park area became shrouded in steam and fog. In this 1950s view from Harringay Up Goods box there are four trains seeking the signalman's attention. The J50 0-6-0T on the Up Goods No.2 has just got the road southwards. Another up goods on the Up Goods No.3 waits to follow, next is a light engine from Hornsey shed on the Engine Line, and at right a transfer move on the Up Viaduct line is approaching. (D.I.D. Loveday / The Gresley

72. Snowclouds provide the atmosphere here as No. 69535 passes the same signals with an up ECS working. (G. Silcock)

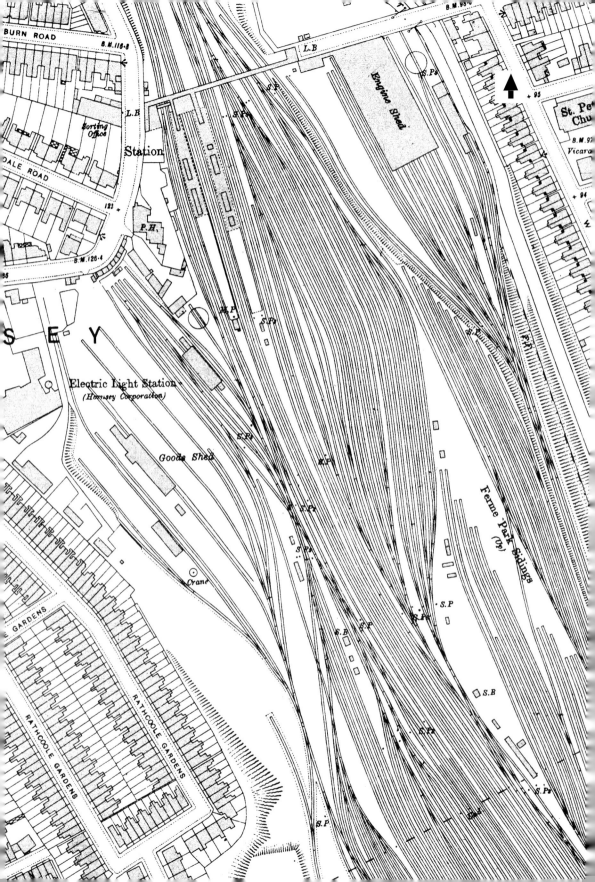

BURN ROAD

B.M.116·8

L.B

Sorting
Office

L.B

Station

DALE ROAD

123

P.H.

B.M.126·4

36

S E Y

Electric Light Station
(Hornsey Corporation)

Goods Shed

Crane

GARDENS

RATHCOOLE GARDENS

RATHCOOLE GARDENS

L.B

B.M.95·

Engine Shed

S.P.

S.P.

S.P.

+ 95

St. Pe
Chu

B.M.9

Vicar

+ 94

S.P.

S.P.

S.P.

S.P.

S.P.

S.P.

S.P.

S.P.

S.P.

S.P.

S.P.

S.B. S.P.

S.P.

S.B.

Ferme Park Sidings
(Up)

S.P.

S.P.

FERME PARK

73. In the foreground of this late-GNR period view from the 'Hog's Back' is Ferme Park Down Yard, which opened in 1887 with 12 doubled-ended sidings, and had been expanded to 24 by 1913. In the c1931 LNER improvements a further 11-road dead-end 'Low Level' yard was added on the west side. The Up Yard opened in 1888, and was greatly expanded in the 1890s. These yards were mainly concerned with the heavy bulk traffic, principally coal, which arrived in the Up Yard in a never-ending sequence of trains from New England and beyond, and left in local workings to King's Cross Goods Yard and other coal depots, notably those in South London reached via the Snow Hill line. The Down Yard dealt with the returning coal empties. In 1955, when the Up and Down yards were each handling some 800 wagons a day, an Eastern Region report recommended a new hump yard here. It was fortunate that this was not proceeded with as in 1966 most of the coal traffic was diverted from the GN to the Midland. The old yards were then lifted. A new 15-road 'Ferme Park Down Sidings' yard opened on the down side in 1974 as part of the new ECML carriage servicing facilities. The Up Yard site was given over to the new Hornsey EMU depot. (D. Gilbert collection)

1913 Ordnace Survey map showing Hornsey station and the north end of Ferme Park yards. Hornsey was one of the original August 1850 stations, the first station out of London. However it was a very last-minute addition, only being decided on in July 1850. The station building (no photographs known) was in a yard off Tottenham Lane, immediately north of the Railway Hotel public house. The down platform was at the same mileage as later, but the up platform was staggered to the south. It was replaced by an up island opposite the down on quadrupling in 1870/1, with the 'three lines between the platforms' arrangement also introduced at Wood Green at this date. As late as the 1870s the station was still surrounded by fields on the east side, but in the '80s and '90s the whole area was transformed. The GNR tipped fill over a large area to make up ground for the Ferme Park marshalling yards, needed to relieve the congested yards at Finsbury Park; and the housing developers covered the remaining spaces with monotonous streets of terraced housing for city clerks and others of 'middling' sort. The station itself was transformed in 1900 when the new Down Slow No.2 and Down Goods lines were laid to the west of the down platform, requiring the removal of the 1850 main buildings. A new overhead booking office was built, with a lengthy new footbridge giving access from both sides of the line; and the down platform became an island with new buildings and canopy. In the early years there had been modest goods facilities alongside the station, but these fell victim to the line widenings, and by the 1890s the large new goods yard seen here had been provided on the down side south of the station. It was the most substantial yard at any of the main line suburban stations, with two goods sheds. Closure to public goods traffic was effected on 7th April 1975.

74. Those photographers who secured permission to walk over the viaduct lines were able to get a better view of the south end of the up yard, which consisted of three groups of dead-end sidings known as the 'Top', 'Klondyke', and 'Harringay' yards. In this 10th May 1960 view, N2 69529 passes with an ECS working on the Up Slow. The lines to the loco shed are seen at far right. (P.H. Groom)

75. The GNR signal gantries that survived into the 1970s may have seemed admirable enough – but some of their predecessors from the 1880s were in a yet more marvellous class! This is Ferme Park on 12th June 1900, viewed from Hornsey Goods Yard throat. NER Q class 4-4-0 No.1875 had brought in a special troop train from the north. The original Ferme Park North Up box (replaced in 1911) is seen at left, the more familiar Ferme Park North Down (1893-1974) at right. (The Gresley Society)

HORNSEY

76. Some time in the late 1890s a lucky photographer captured this all-action view with Stirling single No.774 on the Down Fast overtaking a suburban train on the Down Slow headed by G3 0-4-4T No.695. The down platform is seen in its pre-1900 form, with rear wall, and behind it is the earlier of the two down side goods sheds. The roof of Hornsey No.1 box can be seen above the trains. (J.E. Connor collection)

77. Conveniently taken from the same spot, this late GNR period view shows the down platform in its post-1900 form, with the Down Slow No.2 line serving its west side. The up signals have become decidedly stumpier! Large Atlantic No.1459 (built 1910) heads the 9.50am from King's Cross. (The Gresley Society)

78. Everything seen in this Edwardian postcard view dates from the 1900 rebuilding. The road side buildings (which still existed in 2008) comprised a covered stairway up to the footbridge, and a parcels office under the stairs with covered road vehicle loading bay behind, accessed between the gateposts at centre. (P. Laming collection)

79. This northward view dates from 1971, when things were looking rather shabby. The up platform canopy and buildings dated from 1870/1 (but were lengthened in 1900); the down platform buildings and canopy were wholly new in 1900. All these buildings and canopies, plus the 1900 overhead booking office, were demolished around 1975, when the platforms were reduced to single-sided (the right hand side of each as seen here), serving the Down Slow No.1 and Up Slow. A small new waiting/canopy block was erected on each platform in lieu, similar to those at Harringay; however Hornsey did get a proper new booking office building on the footbridge. (J.E. Connor)

80.   Class N2 0-6-2T No. 69591 departs from Hornsey with a Hatfield service on the afternoon of 8th May 1959. The 1900 footbridge had been covered throughout, but its eastern end had to be removed altogether following bomb damage. After several years in which passengers from the east side were forced to divert via Turnpike Lane, the missing spans were replaced but in uncovered form. (P.H. Groom)

81.   The dual nature of the GN main line is highlighted in this 1950s view from Hornsey station footbridge. Class A4 4-6-2 No. 60021 *Wild Swan* thunders past Hornsey No.2 box on the Up Fast, whilst WD 2-8-0 90000 clanks by with a coal train on the Up Goods ready to stop in the Ferme Park Up Yard reception roads. (D.I.D. Loveday / The Gresley Society)

82.   This is Hornsey Loco Shed shortly after opening in 1899. There had long been ideas of building another shed in London to relieve 'Top Shed', and this site was chosen in 1892. The 8-road shed housed locos for the yard shunting and the cross-London goods workings, and also shared the suburban passenger workings with Top Shed. Additionally locos from Peterborough and beyond were serviced here, before crossing via the viaduct lines to the Down Yard to return with a down goods. The coal stage and water tank are seen at right. (J.E. Connor collection)

83.   What the residents didn't like! Even in the earliest years there were complaints, for Wightman Road was not an industrial working-class community inured to putting up with such things. The nearest houses were only 25 yards from the shed. BR made further attempts to mitigate the problem, but 'clean air' only arrived with dieselisation in 1961. After closing as a loco shed around 1970, the building was converted to serve as an Overhead Line Maintenance Depot, and was still in use as such during 2008. (D.I.D. Loveday / The Gresley Society)

84.   Here we can enjoy the splendid sight of Ivatt Class C1 Atlantic No. 4439 storming past the gantry carrying Wood Green No.1's (down) home signals with No.3's distants in LNER days. (The Gresley Society)

85.   In this early 1960s view, Brush type 2 No. D5586 on a down Cambridge train passes the same gantry as the Atlantic in picture 84 and overtakes a classmate on a down main line suburban service. The train indicators to the right of the frame were placed there to help staff crossing the line. They dated back to Great Northern days. (G. Silcock)

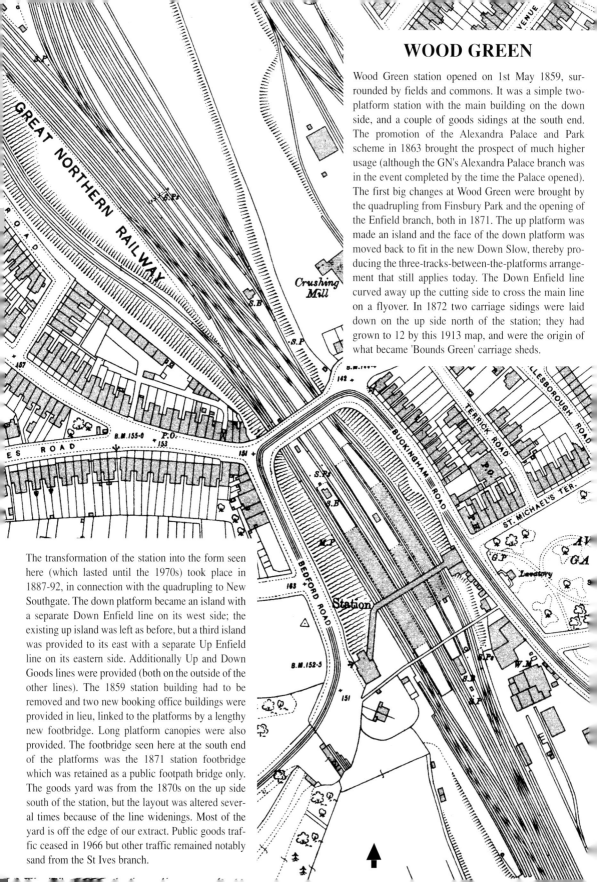

WOOD GREEN

Wood Green station opened on 1st May 1859, surrounded by fields and commons. It was a simple two-platform station with the main building on the down side, and a couple of goods sidings at the south end. The promotion of the Alexandra Palace and Park scheme in 1863 brought the prospect of much higher usage (although the GN's Alexandra Palace branch was in the event completed by the time the Palace opened). The first big changes at Wood Green were brought by the quadrupling from Finsbury Park and the opening of the Enfield branch, both in 1871. The up platform was made an island and the face of the down platform was moved back to fit in the new Down Slow, thereby producing the three-tracks-between-the-platforms arrangement that still applies today. The Down Enfield line curved away up the cutting side to cross the main line on a flyover. In 1872 two carriage sidings were laid down on the up side north of the station; they had grown to 12 by this 1913 map, and were the origin of what became 'Bounds Green' carriage sheds.

The transformation of the station into the form seen here (which lasted until the 1970s) took place in 1887-92, in connection with the quadrupling to New Southgate. The down platform became an island with a separate Down Enfield line on its west side; the existing up island was left as before, but a third island was provided to its east with a separate Up Enfield line on its eastern side. Additionally Up and Down Goods lines were provided (both on the outside of the other lines). The 1859 station building had to be removed and two new booking office buildings were provided in lieu, linked to the platforms by a lengthy new footbridge. Long platform canopies were also provided. The footbridge seen here at the south end of the platforms was the 1871 station footbridge which was retained as a public footpath bridge only. The goods yard was from the 1870s on the up side south of the station, but the layout was altered several times because of the line widenings. Most of the yard is off the edge of our extract. Public goods traffic ceased in 1966 but other traffic remained notably sand from the St Ives branch.

86.   No views of Wood Green in its pre-1890 state seem to be available, so we start with this Edwardian postcard scene looking south from the road bridge. A down main line suburban service is at the Down Slow platform. 'Down Box No.3' dated from 1887. Behind is the snaking 1890 covered footbridge and (right) the rear of the 1890 down side booking office building. The Up Fast / Up Slow platform had only a short canopy, as few trains stopped on the Up Fast; anyone wanting to board an up train would go to the Up Slow / Up Enfield island. (J.E. Connor collection)

Extract from the GNR suburban timetable of 1910

87. In this view, again dating from the 1900s, we are looking over the Up Slow / Up Enfield island towards the 1890 up side booking office building. Although the station had been formally renamed 'Wood Green (Alexandra Park)' in 1864, the suffix was not always shown by the GNR, as is evident from this nameboard which probably dated from 1890. (J.E. Connor collection)

PLATFORM. ADMIT ONE
WOOD GREEN (ALEXANDRA PARK)
THE HOLDER IS PROHIBITED FROM ENTERING THE COMPANY'S TRAINS.
1D
NOT TRANSFERABLE.
FOR CONDITIONS SEE BACK
L. N. E. R.
6347

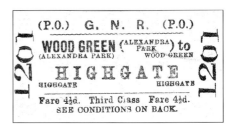

(P.O.) G. N. R. (P.O.)
WOOD GREEN (ALEXANDRA PARK) to WOOD GREEN
(ALEXANDRA PARK)
HIGHGATE
HIGHGATE   HIGHGATE
Fare 4½d. Third Class Fare 4½d.
SEE CONDITIONS ON BACK.
1201   1201

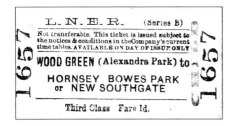

L. N. E. R. (Series B)
Not transferable. This ticket is issued subject to the notices & conditions in the Company's current time tables. AVAILABLE ON DAY OF ISSUE ONLY
WOOD GREEN (Alexandra Park) to
HORNSEY BOWES PARK or NEW SOUTHGATE
Third Class Fare 1d.
1657   1657

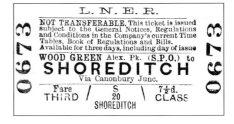

L. N. E. R.
NOT TRANSFERABLE. This ticket is issued subject to the General Notices, Regulations and Conditions in the Company's current Time Tables, Book of Regulations and Bills. Available for three days, including day of issue
WOOD GREEN Alex. Pk. (S.P.O.) to
SHOREDITCH
Via Canonbury Junc.
Fare   S
THIRD / 20 \ 7½d.
          SHOREDITCH   CLASS
0673   0673

88. In contrast to the Great Northern, British Railways was pleased to provide running in boards with the suffix, and no brackets! Here we look east from the down platform towards the large houses in Buckingham Road. At top left are the Great Eastern Railway staff cottages in Bridge Road, the GER having their station nearby at Palace Gates. The station was officially renamed 'Wood Green' on 18th March 1971. (J.E. Connor)

LONDON, FINSBURY PARK, WOOD GREEN, NEW BARNET, HATFIELD, and HITCHIN.

Down. — **Week Days.**

Miles from King's Cross.	Down.	mrn	mrn	mrn		mrn	mrn	mrn	mrn	mrn	mrn	mrn	mrn		mrn	mru	mrn	mrn	mrn	mrn		mrn	mrn		mrn	mrn	mrn	mrn	mrn	mrn	E	mrn
	Moorgate Street....dep.	..	..	..	..	..	..	..	6 51	..	..	7 27	..	..	7 32	7 39	..	..	..	8 38	..	8 49	..		S	9 15	..	..	1011	..	10 42	..
	Aldersgate and Barbican	..	..	..	..	..	..	..	..	..	..	7 29	..	..	..	7 41	..	..	..	8 40	..	8 51	..		..	..	..	..	..	..	10 44	..
	Farringdon & H. Holborn	..	..	..	..	..	..	..	6 55	..	..	7 31	..	..	7 36	7 43	..	..	..	8 43	..	8 53	..		..	9 19	..	..	1015	..	10 46	..
	King's Cross (Met.)......	..	..	..	..	..	..	..	6 59	..	..	7 35	..	..	7 40	7 47	..	..	..	8 47	..	8 57	..		..	9 23	..	..	1019	..	10 50	..
	LONDON (King's Cross)..	4 20	5 5	5 22	..	6 15	..	..	7 2	7 10	..	7 38	7 45	..	7 42	7 51	8 5	..	8 45	8 51	..	9 0	9 17		..	9 26	..	1020	1022	..	10 52	11 0
—	Finsbury Park......arr.	4 25	5 11	5 27	..	6 20	..	..	7 8	7 15	..	7 43	7 51	..	..	7 56	8 10	..	8 51	8 56	..	9 5	9 22		..	9 31	..	1027	..	..	..	11 5
—	Mls Broad Street ¶..dep.	..	..	..	..	..	..	6 41	..	..	..	..	..	..	..	..	..	8 9	..	..	..	..	..		..	..	9 48	..	..	1027	..	..
—	2 Dalston Junction...	..	..	..	..	..		6 48	..	..	..	..	..	..	..	..	..	8 17	..	..	..	..	..		..	..	9 55	..	..	1032	..	..
—	3 Canonbury.........	..	..	..	..	..		6 52	..	..	..	..	..	..	..	..	..	8 21	..	..	..	..	..		..	..	9 59	..	..	1036	..	..
—	4¼ Finsbury Park..arr.	..	..	..	..	..		6 56	..	..	..	..	..	..	..	..	..	8 27	..	..	..	..	..		..	..	10 3	..	..	1042	..	..
2½	Finsbury Park......dep.	4 27	5 13	5 29	..	6 22	Runs to Baldock (arrives 7 28 mrn.), see page 866.	6 58	7 10	7 18	7 35	7 44	7 53	..	..	7 57	8 13	8 30	8 52	8 59	..	9 8	9 23	Runs to Dunstable, see page 865.	..	9 33	10 6	1031	..	1044	..	11 7
3¼	Harringay...............	4 30	..	5 32	..	6 25		7 1	..	7 21	..	7 47	..	..	..	8 0	..	8 33	..	9 2	..	9 11	..		..	9 36	10 9	..	..	1047	..	1110
4½	Hornsey..................	4 33	..	5 34	..	6 29		7 3	..	7 25	..	7 49	..	..	..	8 2	..	8 35	..	9 4	..	9 13	..		..	9 38	1011	..	..	1049	..	1113
5	Wood Green **A**........	4 36	..	5 37	..	6 32		7 6	..	7 29	..	7 52	..	..	..	8 5	8 19	8 38	..	9 7	..	9 16	..		..	9 41	1014	..	..	1052	..	1116
6½	New Southgate **B**......	4 40	..	5 41	..	6 38		7 11	7 19	7 34	7 44	7 56	..	..	..	8 9	8 24	8 42	..	9 11	..	9 20	..		..	9 45	1018	..	..	1057	..	1121
8¼	Oakleigh Park **C**.......	4 45	..	5 46	..	6 43		7 17	7 24	7 39	..	8 1	..	..	..	8 14	8 29	8 47	..	9 16	..	9 25	..		..	9 50	1024	..	..	11 3	..	1126
9¼	**New Barnet**...........	4 47	..	5 48	..	6 45		7 19	7 31	7 43	7 50	8 3	..	..	..	8 17	8 32	8 49	..	9 19	..	9 27	9 35		..	9 53	1026	1042	..	11 7	..	1131
10¾	Hadley Wood.............	..	..	..	..	..		..	..	7 47	..	..	..	..	..	..	8 36	..	..	9 23	..	..	..		..	9 57	..	1046	..	1111	..	1135
12¾	Potters Bar **D**..........	..	5 29	..	..	..		..	7 39	7 52	..	..	..	..	..	..	8 41	..	..	9 28	..	..	..		..	10 1	..	1051	..	1116	..	1140
14¾	Brookman's Park.........	..	..	..	..	..		..	..	7 56	..	..	..	..	..	..	8 45	..	..	9 33	..	..	..		..	..	..	1055	..	..	..	1144
17¾	**Hatfield 865**...... arr.	..	5 36	..	..	..		..	7 47	8 2	..	..	8 16	..	..	..	8 51	..	9 15	9 38	..	..	9 46		..	..	..	11 1	..	..	..	1152
	Hatfield 865...... dep.	..	5 39	..	..	..	6 46	..	7 48	8 6	..	..	8 21	..	..	..	8 53	..	9 16	..	..	..	9 51		9 58	..	..	11 3	..	..	..	..
20¼	Welwyn Garden City....	..	5 46	..	..	..	6 52	..	7 53	8 12	..	..	8 27	..	..	..	8 59	..	..	..	..	..	9 57		10 4	..	..	11 9	..	..	..	..
22	Welwyn North...........	..	..	..	..	..	6 56	..	..	8 16	..	..	..	..	..	..	9 3	..	..	..	..	..	..		10 8	..	..	1113	..	..	..	..
25	Knebworth...............	..	5 54	..	..	..	7 3	..	..	8 22	..	..	..	..	..	..	9 10	..	..	..	..	..	..		1015	..	..	1120	..	..	..	..
28½	Stevenage 866 [817, 866	..	6 1	..	..	..	7 9	..	..	8 28	..	..	..	..	..	..	9 16	..	..	..	..	..	..		1021	..	..	1127	..	..	..	..
32	**Hitchin** 683, **810**, arr.	..	6 7	..	..	..	7 15	..	..	8 34	..	..	8 43	..	..	..	9 22	..	9 34	..	..	..	..		1027	..	..	1133	..	..	..	..

Down. — **Week Days**—*Continued.*

Down.	mrn	aft	mrn	S	S	aft	S		aft	S	aft	aft		aft	aft	S	aft		aft	aft	aft		S	aft	aft		aft	aft		aft	S
Moorgate Street.........dep.	..	S	E	1143	12 0	E	12 6	..	S	1226	S	..	..	S	..	1 0	S	..	S	S	E	..	1 32	..	S	..	S	E	..	S	2 6
Aldersgate and Barbican......	..	..	..	1145	12 2	..	12 8	..	..	1228	..	..	..	..	..	1 2	..	..	..	..	..	..	1 34	..	..	..	..	..	..	..	2 8
Farringdon and High Holborn	..	..	..	1147	12 4	..	1210	..	..	1230	..	..	..	..	..	1 4	..	..	..	..	..	..	1 36	..	..	..	..	..	..	..	2 10
King's Cross (Met.)............	..	..	..	1151	12 8	..	1214	..	..	1234	..	..	..	..	..	1 8	..	..	..	..	..	..	1 40	..	..	..	..	..	..	..	2 14
LONDON (King's Cross)......	1130	Runs to Cambrige (arr. 1 45 aft.), see page 866.	1145	1155	1211	1217	1217	..	1230	1237	1240	1245	..	1258	1 5	..	1 23	..	..	1 33	..	..	..	1 45	1 50	..	..	..	..	..	2 18
Finsbury Park...........arr.	1136		1150	12 0	1216	1222	1222	..	..	1242	..	1250	..	1 3	1 10	1 16	..	..	..	1 38	..	..	1 47	1 51	1 55	..	..	..	..	..	2 23
Broad Street ¶........dep.	..		..	..	..	..	..	..	..	..	..	..	..	..	..	..	..	..	1 26	..	..	..	..	..	..	..	1 50	..	..	..	..
Dalston Junction..........	..		..	..	..	..	..	..	..	..	..	..	..	..	..	..	..	..	1 31	..	..	..	..	..	..	..	1 55	..	..	..	..
Canonbury.................	..		..	..	..	..	..	..	..	..	..	..	..	..	..	..	..	..	1 34	..	..	..	..	..	..	..	1 59	..	..	..	..
Finsbury Park.........arr.	..		..	..	..	..	..	..	..	..	..	..	..	..	..	..	..	..	1 38	..	..	..	..	..	..	..	2 3	..	..	..	..
Finsbury Park..........dep.	1137		1152	12 1	1217	1223	1223	..	..	1243	..	1251	..	1 5	1 11	1 18	..	..	1 39	1 40	1 41	..	1 48	1 52	1 56	..	2 5	2 16	..	2 17	2 26
Harringay......................	..		1155	12 4	1220	1226	1226	..	..	1246	..	1254	..	..	..	..	1 30	..	..	1 43	1 44	..	1 51	..	..	..	2 8	2 19	..	2 20	2 29
Hornsey.......................	..		1157	12 6	1222	1228	1228	..	..	1248	..	1256	..	..	..	..	1 32	..	..	1 45	1 46	..	1 53	..	..	..	2 10	2 21	..	2 22	2 32
Wood Green **A**..............	..		12 0	12 9	1225	1231	1231	..	..	1251	..	1259	..	..	..	1 24	1 35	..	..	1 48	1 49	..	1 56	..	2 1	..	2 14	2 24	..	2 25	2 35
New Southgate **B**...........	..		12 4	1213	..	1235	1235	..	..	1255	..	1 3	..	1 12	..	1 29	1 39	..	..	1 53	1 53	..	..	..	2 5	..	2 18	2 28	..	2 29	2 40
Oakleigh Park **C**...........	..		12 9	1217	..	1240	1240	..	..	1 0	..	1 8	..	1 17	..	1 34	1 44	..	..	1 58	1 59	..	..	..	2 10	..	2 24	2 33	..	2 34	2 45
New Barnet................	..		1212	1220	..	1243	1246	..	..	1 2	..	1 11	..	1 19	..	1 37	1 46	..	1K51	2 0	2 5	..	..	..	2 12	..	2 27	2 36	..	2 37	2 47
Hadley Wood..................	..		1216	1224	..	1247	1250	..	..	..	..	1 15	..	..	1 25	..	..	..	2 0	..	2 9	..	..	..	..	..	..	2 40	..	2 41	..
Potters Bar **D**..............	..		1221	1229	..	1252	1255	..	..	..	..	1 19	..	..	1 30	..	..	..	2 5	..	2 14	..	..	..	..	..	..	2 45	..	2 46	..
Brookman's Park..............	..		..	..	..	..	..	..	..	..	..	1S25	..	..	1 35	..	..	..	..	..	..	..	..	..	..	..	..	..	..	2 50	..
Hatfield 865........... arr.	12 1		..	..	..	..	..	..	..	..	1 7	1S31	..	..	1 44	..	..	..	..	..	..	..	..	2 15	..	..	..	..	..	2 56	..
Hatfield 865........... dep.	12 3	1210	..	..	..	..	..	..	..	..	1 10	..	..	..	1 46	..	..	..	..	..	..	..	..	2 17	..	..	..	..	..	..	..
Welwyn Garden City........	..	1216	..	..	..	..	..	..	1 0	..	..	..	..	..	1X59	..	..	..	..	..	..	..	..	2 23	..	..	..	..	..	..	..
Welwyn North.................	..	1220	..	..	..	..	..	..	1 4	..	..	..	..	..	2 3	..	..	..	..	..	..	..	..	2 27	..	..	..	..	..	..	..
Knebworth.....................	..	1227	..	..	..	..	..	..	1 12	..	..	..	..	..	2 11	..	..	..	..	..	..	..	..	2 34	..	..	..	..	..	..	..
Stevenage **866**...........[866	..	1234	..	..	..	..	..	..	1 19	..	..	..	..	..	2 18	..	..	..	..	..	..	..	..	2 41	..	..	..	..	..	..	..
Hitchin 683, **810**, 817, arr.	1222	1240	..	..	..	..	..	..	1 25	..	1 30	..	..	..	2 24	..	..	..	..	..	..	..	..	2 47	..	..	..	..	..	..	..

¶ Nearly all Trains call at Shoreditch 2 minutes and Haggerston 5 minutes after leaving Broad Street.

Extract from the LNER suburban timetable of 1930.

89. Here we see the 1890 up side booking office building in Buckingham Road in the 1960s. The Italianate style was somewhat unusual at this late a date, however both buildings at Wood Green are clearly modelled on that provided in 1873 at Alexandra Palace. (J.E. Connor)

90. This is the 1890 down side booking office. The building was closed in 1967 and this photograph was taken soon after. There is still access to the station from this side of the line, but this attractive building has long been swept away. (J.E. Connor)

91. Scenes of destruction like this could be witnessed at most stations on the line in the mid-1970s. Here the Up Slow / Up Enfield island is being demolished (in the new layout the Up Enfield and Up Slow met north of the platform). All the GN buildings at Wood Green were demolished in 1974 except for the up side booking office.
(G.L. Pring / Railway Record of the British Isles)

ALEXANDRA PALACE

92. We end with the same view that we started with, but this time showing the new railway created in the 1970s. The photograph was taken on 16th May 1982 whilst men were busy taking down the 'Wood Green' signs and putting up 'Alexandra Palace' signs, in line with a further renaming prompted by the reviving of the Palace. (P. Kay)

NORTH OF WOOD GREEN

93. In this view from around 1925, Ivatt Large Atlantic No.1427N largely obfuscates the southern portals of Wood Green (originally 'Tottenham') tunnel as it passes Wood Green Tunnel Box with an up Pullman service. (The Gresley Society)

NEW SOUTHGATE

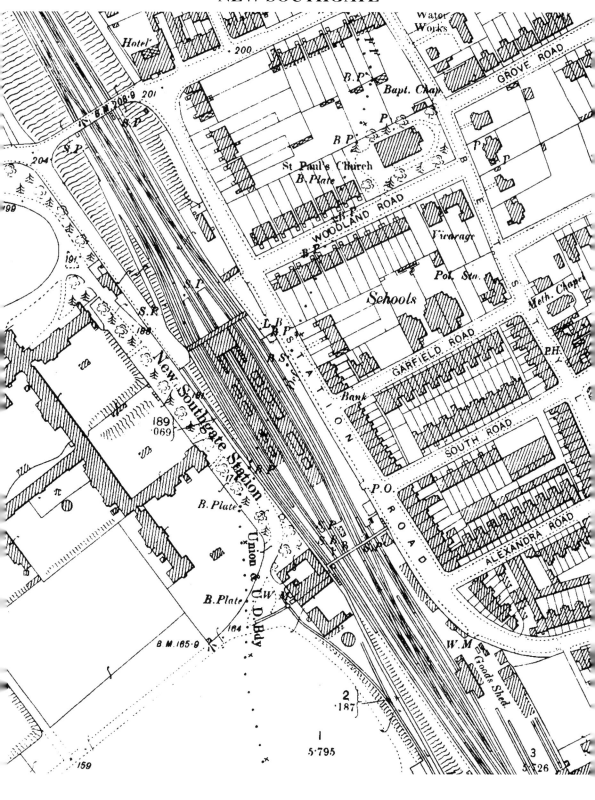

94.   The 1890 passenger facilities are seen in this northward view from the late GNR period. At this time the platform nameboards read 'New Southgate & Friern Barnet for Colney Hatch' (as did the replacement boards put up by the LNER in the 1920s). Yet in timetables the '& Friern Barnet' did not appear until 1923, nor was it seen on GNR tickets. (J.E. Connor collection)

New Southgate station opened with the line on 7th August 1850, as 'Colney Hatch & Southgate' (altered to 'Southgate & Colney Hatch' in 1855, 'New Southgate & Colney Hatch' in 1876, and 'New Southgate (for Colney Hatch)' in 1883). It was provided to serve the new Middlesex County Lunatic Asylum then under construction adjacent, but a new suburb soon sprung up to the east of the line to produce more traffic. Until the 1880s the station had staggered platforms, the down at the same mileage as later, the up further south with the main station building behind it in Station Road (opposite the Alexandra Road junction here). The station was completely reconstructed in the form seen here in 1889/90, in connection with the main line quadrupling between Wood Green and New Barnet. The down platform was widened to an island with the new Down Slow on its west side, and a wholly new up island was built opposite. The principal new station entrance was more than 200 yards north of the old, from a small courtyard in Station Road via a new covered footbridge to an overhead booking office. A second entrance was available at the west end of the footbridge, from a new 'Station Approach' road. The old station

footbridge at the south end was retained as a footpath bridge only. Lengthy goods loading platforms were also provided on both sides. The goods yard (closed to public traffic 1970) remained on the up side south of the station. The Gasworks on the down side was part of the Asylum, its sidings accessed from the wagon turntable under the old footbridge. The up side Gasworks belonged to the Southgate & Colney Hatch Gas Light & Coke Co. The map dates from 1894.

95. 4-4-2T No.1534 passes under the Friern Barnet Road overbridge (at top of map extract) with a down main line suburban working in late GNR days. The remodelling of around 1890 saw four new signal boxes opened, of which No.2 (up) and No.3 (down) were unusually located in the bridge arches as seen here. No.1 box (down) was well south of the station (see map), No.4 (up) at the south end of the up platform is glimpsed at far right in picture 94. In 1925 a major rationalisation was effected under which No.4 took sole control. (The Gresley Society)

MOORGATE, KING'S CROSS, BROAD STREET, ALEXANDRA PALACE, HIGH BARNET, HERTFORD (North), HATFIELD and HITCHIN

WEEKDAYS

		SO				SO		
		p.m.	p.m.		p.m.	p.m.		p.m.
1	MOORGATE .. .. dep.	Service	..	..	..	..		..
2	Aldersgate and Barbican .. .. ,,	temporarily	..	..	..	..		..
3	Farringdon .. .. ,,	suspended	..	..	..	..		..
4	Kings Cross (Metropolitan) .. .. ,,		..	..	..	..		..
5	KING'S CROSS (L.N.E.R.) .. dep.	1 43	..	1 50	..	2 5		..
6	BROAD STREET — — — dep.	Service	..	..	..	..		..
7	Shoreditch .. .. ,,	temporarily	..	..	..	..		..
8	Dalston Junction .. .. .. ,,	suspended	..	..	..	..		..
9	Canonbury.. .. .. ,,		..	..	..	..		..
10	FINSBURY PARK .. .. { arr.	1 49	..	1 56	..	2 12	—	—
11	{ dep.	1 51	..	1 57	..	2 13	2 13	2 14	..	2 15
12	Stroud Green — — dep.	..	..	..	..	..	—	—	2 18
13	Crouch End .. .. .. ,,	..	..	..	..	..	—	—	2 21
14	Highgate .. .. .. ,,	..	..	..	..	..	—	—	2 25
15	Cranley Gardens .. .. dep.	..	..	..	..	..	—	—	2 28
16	Muswell Hill .. .. ,,	..	..	..	..	..	—	—	2 30
17	ALEXANDRA PALACE .. .. arr.	..	..	..	..	..	—	—	2 33
18	{ Highgate — — dep.	..	..	..	..	..	—	—	2 27
19	{ East Finchley — — arr.	..	..	..	..	..	—	—	2 30
20	{ Finchley Central .. .. ,,	..	..	..	..	..	—	—	2 33
21	A { Mill Hill East .. .. ,,	..	..	..	..	..	—	—	2 44
22	{ West Finchley — — ,,	..	..	..	..	..	—	—	2 35
23	{ Woodside Pk. for N. Finchley — ,,	..	..	..	..	..	—	—	2 37
24	{ Totteridge and Whetstone — ,,	..	..	..	..	..	—	—	2 40
25	{ HIGH BARNET .. .. .. arr.	..	..	..	..	..	—	—	2 44
26	Harringay — — dep.	—	2 0	—	2 16	—	..	..	..
27	Hornsey .. .. .. ,,	—	2 2	—	2 18	—	..	..	..
28	Wood Green (Alexandra Park) — ,,	—	2 5	—	2 21	2 21	..	..	..
29	Bowes Park — — dep.	—	2 8	—	2 24	—	..	..	..
30	Palmers Green and Southgate — ,,	—	2 11	—	2 27	—	..	..	..
31	Winchmore Hill — — ,,	—	2 14	—	2 30	—	..	..	..
32	Grange Park — — ,,	—	2 16	—	2 32	—	..	..	..
33	Enfield Chase — — ,,	—	2 19	—	2 35	—	..	..	..
34	Gordon Hill — — ,,	—	2 23	—	2 39	—	..	..	..
35	Crews Hill — — ,,	—	—	—	2 43	—	..	..	..
36	Cuffley and Goff's Oak — ,,	—	—	—	2 48	—	..	..	..
37	Bayford .. .. ,,	—	—	—	..	—	..	..	..
38	HERTFORD (North) .. .. arr.	—	—	—	..	—	..	..	..
39	New Southgate and Friern Barnet.. dep.	..	..	—	2 25	—	..	..	..
40	Oakleigh Park for East Barnet — ,,	..	..	—	2 30	—	..	..	..
41	New Barnet .. .. .. ,,	..	..	—	2 33	—	..	..	..
42	Hadley Wood .. .. .. ,,	..	..	—	2 37	—	..	..	..
43	Potters Bar and South Mimms.. .. ,,	..	..	—	2 31	2 42	..	..	..
44	Brookman's Park .. .. ,,	..	..	—	2 35	—	..	..	..
45	Hatfield .. .. .. { arr.	..	..	2 16	—	2 41	—	..	..
46	{ dep.	..	..	2 18	—	2 43	—	..	..
47	Welwyn Garden City —	..	..	2 24	—	2 50	—	..	..
48	Welwyn North — — ..	..	..	2 29	—	2 55	—	..	..
49	Knebworth	..	..	2 36	—	3 3	—	..	..
50	Stevenage	..	..	2 43	—	3 12	—	..	..
51	HITCHIN .. .. .. arr.	..	..	2 50	—	3 19	—	..	..

A Electric service. Passengers for these stations change at Highgate.
SO Saturdays only.

MOORGATE, KING'S CROSS, BROAD STREET, ALEXANDRA PALACE, HIGH BARNET, HERTFORD (North), HATFIELD and HITCHIN

WEEKDAYS—continued

	SO				SO					SX		
	p.m.	p.m.	p.m.		p.m.	p.m.	p.m.		p.m.		p.m.	p.m.	p.m.
1	..	..	—	..	..	..	..	—	..		..	..	..
2	..	..	—	..	..	..	..	—	..		..	..	..
3	..	..	—	..	..	..	..	—	..		..	..	..
4	..	..	—	..	..	..	..	—	..		..	..	..
5	2 35	2 38	..	..	2 50	3 0	..	3 5	..	3 8	..	3 21	..	..	3 34	..	..
6	—	—	—	..	..	—	—	—	..		..	..	..
7	—	—	—	..	..	—	—	—	..		..	..	..
8	—	—	—	..	..	—	—	—	..		..	..	..
9	—	—	—	..	..	—	—	—	..		..	..	..
10	2 41	2 44	—	..	2 56	3 6	—	—	..	3 14	..	3 27	..	..	3 40	..	..
11	2 42	2 46	—	..	2 57	3 7	—	..	..	3 15	..	3 29	3 42	3 42	..	..	3 45
12	..	..	2 53	..	..	..	..	—	..	3 18	..	..	..	—	3 48
13	..	..	2 56	..	..	..	..	—	..	3 21	..	..	..	—	3 51
14	..	..	3 0	..	..	..	..	—	..	3 25	..	..	..	—	3 55
15	..	..	3 3	..	..	..	..	—	..	3 28	..	..	..	—	3 58
16	..	..	3 5	..	..	..	..	—	..	3 30	..	..	..	—	4 0
17	..	..	3 7	..	..	..	..	—	..	3 34	..	..	..	—	4 3
18	—	—	3 3	..	..	—	—	—	..	3 27	..	..	..	—	3 57
19	—	—	3 6	..	..	—	—	—	..	3 30	..	..	..	—	4 0
20	—	—	3 10	..	..	—	—	—	..	3 33	..	..	..	—	4 4
21	—	—	3 14	..	..	—	—	—	..	3 44	..	..	..	—	4 14
22	—	—	3 19	..	..	—	—	—	..	3 35	..	..	..	—	4 6
23	—	—	3 21	..	..	—	—	—	..	3 37	..	..	..	—	4 8
24	—	—	3 24	..	..	—	—	—	..	3 40	..	..	..	—	4 11
25	—	—	3 28	..	..	—	—	—	..	3 44	..	..	..	—	4 14
26	2 45	2 49	—	..	..	3 0	—	—	..	..	..	..	—	3 45	..
27	2 47	2 51	—	..	..	3 2	—	—	..	..	..	..	—	3 47	..
28	2 50	2 54	—	..	..	3 5	3 12	—	..	..	..	..	3 47	3 50	..
29	..	2 57	—	..	..	3 8	—	—	..	..	..	..	—	3 53	..
30	..	3 0	—	..	..	3 11	—	—	..	..	..	..	—	3 56	..
31	..	3 3	—	..	..	3 14	—	—	..	..	..	..	—	3 59	..
32	..	3 5	—	..	..	3 16	—	—	..	..	..	..	—	4 1	..
33	..	3 8	—	..	..	3 19	—	—	..	..	..	..	—	4 4	..
34	..	3 12	—	..	..	3 23	—	—	..	..	..	..	—	4 8	..
35	..	3 16	—	..	..	—	—	—	..	..	..	..	—	4 12	..
36	..	3 21	—	..	..	—	—	—	..	..	..	..	—	4 17	..
37	..	3 28	—	..	..	—	—	—	..	..	..	..	—	4 24	..
38	..	3 34	—	..	..	—	—	—	..	..	..	..	—	4 30	..
39	2 54	—	—	..	..	3 16	—	—	..	..	..	..	3 51	—	..
40	2 59	—	—	..	..	3 21	—	—	..	..	..	..	3 56	—	..
41	3 2	—	—	..	..	3 24	—	—	..	..	..	..	3 59	—	..
42	3 6	—	—	..	..	3 28	—	—	..	..	..	..	4 3	—	..
43	3 11	—	—	..	..	3 33	—	—	..	..	..	..	4 8	—	..
44	..	—	—	..	..	3 37	—	—	..	..	..	..	—	—	..
45	..	—	—	..	..	3 46	—	—	..	3 54	..	..	—	—	..
46	..	—	—	..	..	—	—	—	..	3 56	..	..	—	—	..
47	..	—	—	..	..	—	—	—	..	4 2	..	..	—	—	..
48	..	—	—	..	..	—	—	—	..	4 6	..	..	—	—	..
49	..	—	—	..	..	—	—	—	..	4 14	..	..	—	—	..
50	..	—	—	..	..	—	—	—	..	4 21	..	..	—	—	..
51	..	—	—	..	3 51	—	—	—	..	4 28	..	..	—	—	..

(column 26–51 headed "Buffet Car")

SO Saturdays only. SX Saturdays excepted.

Extracts from the L N E R timetable of 1941.

96. This is the view looking north around 1970, showing the overhead Booking Office. The station name reverted to plain 'New Southgate' in 1971. (J.E. Connor)

97. The southern two-thirds of the platform canopies and buildings were demolished in summer 1975 and although the booking office was intended for retention it was burnt down in December 1976. Three decades later it still has no proper replacement! As this 2008 view shows, all that remains of the old station today is the bulk of the 1890 footbridge and these very short sections of canopy. (P. Kay)

CEMETERY

98.   The Great Northern London Cemetery Company was established in 1855 to create a cemetery at Southgate to which (using the model of the Brookwood cemetery) burial parties would travel from Kings Cross (see picture 39) by special trains. The cemetery opened in 1861. A line was laid for the company's trains from the New Southgate up sidings directly alongside the GNR up line as far as Brunswick Avenue overbridge, then climbing away up the cutting slope to a private Cemetery station just inside the company's grounds. However the rail service proved a failure, the last regular trains running in 1863. This 1900s view includes the elaborate buildings of the Cemetery station on the left and the main line on the right. The track into the station had been lifted around 1877, but the buildings remained until around 1916 when the company sold off this part of their ground for factory development. (J.E. Connor collection)

99.   In 1922 Cemetery Down box was abolished and Cemetery Up took over the whole layout. Note the removal of the letters UP from the nameboard! The Up box, which lasted until 1973, was unusually constructed on a high brick base. In this 1932 view Class K3 2-6-0 No.153 is passing with the 3.40pm Down Scotch Goods. In the background are the early buildings of the STC (Standard Telephones & Cables) works; the large blocks alongside the railway, familiar to latterday passengers, were erected around 1934. (The Gresley Society)

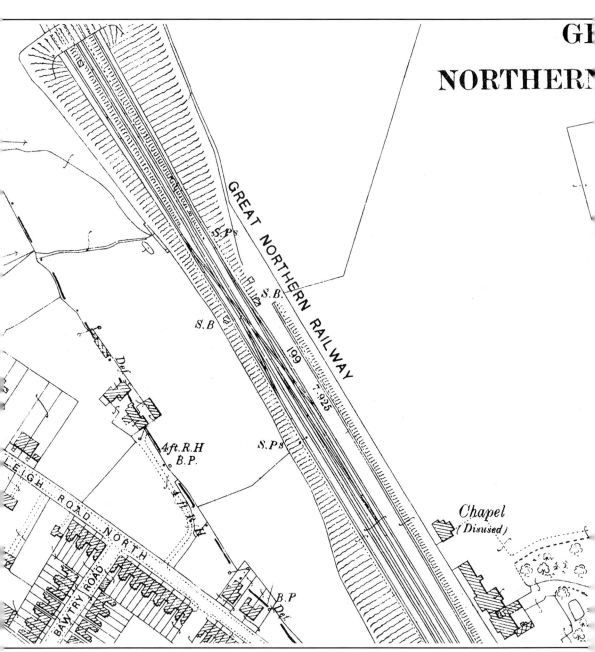

'Cemetery' as a GNR location did not exist until 1878, when a signal box was opened here to control the connection to a new Up Goods line to New Southgate (running on the formation of the Cemetery Co's line for most of the way). Nothing then happened until the main line quadrupling between New Southgate and Oakleigh Park in 1890-92, when the two new signal boxes seen here, Cemetery Down and Cemetery Up, replaced the 1878 box. The existing Up Goods became the Up Slow and a replacement Up Goods was laid outside it. At the top of this extract the southern portals of Barnet tunnel are seen. Here and at Wood Green tunnel, the quadrupling was done by building new single-track bores for the Down Slow and Up Slow either side of the 1850 tunnel. At the bottom right corner of this extract from the Ordnance Survey of 1894 are the Cemetery station buildings, now fenced off from the railway.

OAKLEIGH PARK

100. A down suburban working departs on the Down Fast line in late GNR days, passing under the 'old' footbridge. The Up box seen here was built in 1901 to replace the adjacent 1892 box, for reasons unknown. The down siding is in the foreground. (The Gresley Society)

101. 0-6-0 No.8 pauses at the Up Fast platform below the 1891 footbridge and Booking Office in GNR days. The booking office, entered at footbridge level, was a two-storey structure built on the platform and was not gantried as at other stations. (The Gresley Society)

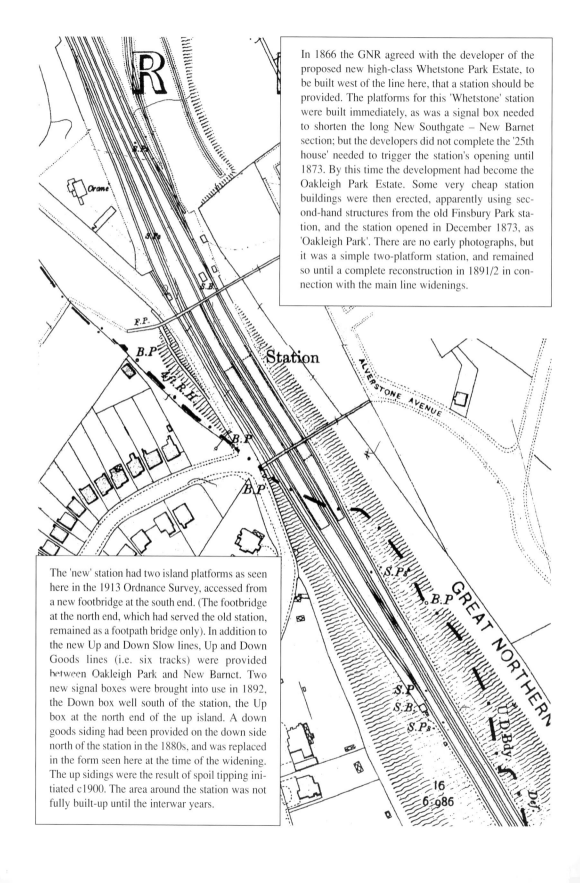

In 1866 the GNR agreed with the developer of the proposed new high-class Whetstone Park Estate, to be built west of the line here, that a station should be provided. The platforms for this 'Whetstone' station were built immediately, as was a signal box needed to shorten the long New Southgate – New Barnet section; but the developers did not complete the '25th house' needed to trigger the station's opening until 1873. By this time the development had become the Oakleigh Park Estate. Some very cheap station buildings were then erected, apparently using second-hand structures from the old Finsbury Park station, and the station opened in December 1873, as 'Oakleigh Park'. There are no early photographs, but it was a simple two-platform station, and remained so until a complete reconstruction in 1891/2 in connection with the main line widenings.

The 'new' station had two island platforms as seen here in the 1913 Ordnance Survey, accessed from a new footbridge at the south end. (The footbridge at the north end, which had served the old station, remained as a footpath bridge only). In addition to the new Up and Down Slow lines, Up and Down Goods lines (i.e. six tracks) were provided between Oakleigh Park and New Barnet. Two new signal boxes were brought into use in 1892, the Down box well south of the station, the Up box at the north end of the up island. A down goods siding had been provided on the down side north of the station in the 1880s, and was replaced in the form seen here at the time of the widening. The up sidings were the result of spoil tipping initiated c1900. The area around the station was not fully built-up until the interwar years.

102.   The LNER added 'For East Barnet' to the station's name in the 1920s, as shown on the new nameboards here. The view was taken from the old footbridge in 1932 and we are looking south. (J.E. Connor collection)

103.   In 1924 both the existing signal boxes were abolished and one new box opened in lieu at the south end of the down platform. However some of the GNR somersaults were still in use at the date of this photograph. (J.E. Connor collection)

104.   Oakleigh Park was resignalled (with colour lights controlled initially from New Barnet), and the signal box abolished, as early as 1970. The Goods lines were taken out of use at the same time. Nevertheless the gaslit station retained a good period atmosphere in the early 1970s. In this southward view the north portals of Barnet tunnel are seen in the distance. (J.E. Connor)

105.   This 1990s view, from the same spot as picture 101, shows the station in its present-day form. In the mid-1970s both footbridges were replaced and the platform buildings and canopies cut back in length, with new valancing. However the 1891 booking office building remains, with a few alterations. (J.E. Connor)

NEW BARNET

The station opened with the line on 7th August 1850, as 'Barnet' (the name was changed in 1884 to avoid confusion with High Barnet). It was 1½ miles from the town, but the surrounding area was about to be developed as the 'Lyonsdown Estate'. The platforms were staggered, the original up platform being the northern half of the later up platform, the down platform was further north with the station buildings situated behind it in Station Approach. The first big changes came in 1877 when, in response to an increase in the number of terminating suburban trains, the up platform was made an island with a bay line on its east side. A new goods yard was also provided on the up side, with access off Lancaster Road (as here). The station and layout were transformed in 1891-6 to the form shown here. The Up and Down Slow lines were put in, plus Up and Down Goods lines to/from Oakleigh Park; this required removal of the existing down platform and the 1850 station building, with a new down island being built opposite the up. A new overhead booking office was provided, accessed from a new covered footbridge which provided a second station entrance on the east side. Only the up platform and the goods yard/shed survived from the old. This 'new station' cost over £15,000 and when Col. Yorke inspected it in March 1896 he had no critical comment to offer, only noting that the new waiting rooms 'leave nothing to be desired'. The large structure in the station yard at the west end of the footbridge was a porte-cochere for carriage folk to alight in the dry. The signal boxes shown here are (south end) New Barnet No.1 (later South) 1895-1970, (south end of up platform) New Barnet No.2 1895-1924, (north end) New Barnet No.3 (later North) 1877-1976. After the 1890s there were no changes of note to the layout or buildings until the 1970s. The map shown here dates from 1913.

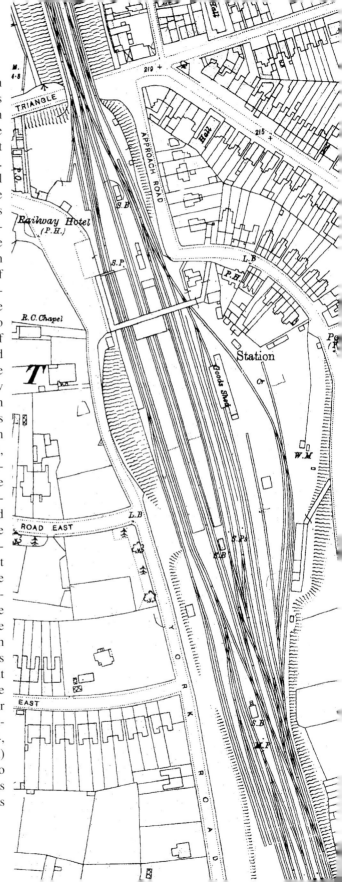

106. In the distance can be seen the original 1850 station building, around 1890 (it was demolished in 1895). It was situated just to the right of the word 'Hotel' on the map extract. (Barnet Museum)

107. Another view of the station prior to the 1890s reconstruction. The photographer is standing on the old down side loading bank platform, which was removed in 1893 to make way for the new down platform. At left is the south end of the 1877 up platform (as today). Single No.231 passes with a down express. The signal box is the 1877-1895 New Barnet South. (E.J. Bedford)

108. This is a late-GNR period view of the station taken from the down side retaining wall, very close to the previous photo location. The Down Goods and Down Slow are in the foreground. The 1895 down platform buildings and canopy on the left contrast with the 1877 up platform canopy. At the right is the 1877 goods shed, which lasted into the 1980s. (The Gresley Society)

109. Following goods closure in 1966, and the end of terminating suburban workings at the same period, the New Barnet layout was ripe for rationalisation. This was effected as early as 1970, when colour-light signalling controlled from a panel in the North box was commissioned. The platform structures were cut back in 1975. The 1895 overhead booking office was intended to remain but was burnt down in 1989. However a replacement single-storey brick building was provided by BR at road level at the west end of the footbridge. This 2008 photograph shows all that now remains of the GNR buildings – the northern ends of the platform canopies and buildings, and the girders that formerly carried the old booking office. (P. Kay)

GREENWOOD

110. Greenwood as a GNR location came into being in 1876 when the signal box (at first called 'Hadley') was opened to control the connection to a new Up Goods line to Barnet. This line became the Up Slow in 1892, in which year a Down Goods was also opened from New Barnet to Greenwood. From then until 1959 this was where the GN's four tracks from London came to an end. This view shows an up Cambridge train passing the box in late GNR days. (The Gresley Society)

111. The LNER bought land in the interwar years for quadrupling from Greenwood to Potters Bar, but the work was not done until 1957-9. New double-track Hadley South, Hadley North, and Potters Bar tunnels, lined with interlocking curved concrete segments, were bored to the west of the 1850 tunnels. The changeovers to the new layout were effected in April-May 1959. Here on 11th April the new Down Slow line behind the box is already in use, but the other lines are still on the old alignments. On 26th/27th April all lines were slewed so that the new tunnels took the Down Slow and Down Fast and the old tunnels the Up Fast and Up Slow. Greenwood box was abolished and New Barnet North began working to the Potters Bar panel box. (J.F. Aylard)

HADLEY WOOD

Hadley Wood station is shown on the 1930 revision map, 2in to 1m. This location began as 'Beech Hill Park' public goods sidings and signal box in 1884, but the name was changed when the passenger station, serving a new housing development, opened on 1st May 1885 (the same day as Harringay). The station was situated between Hadley South and Hadley North tunnels, and had a booking office gantried over the tracks on the north side of the road bridge. A mains crossover was provided in 1900. The signal box was abolished as a block post in 1922/3.

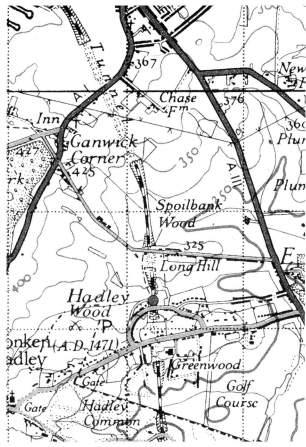

Below : Extract from the British Railways suburban timetable of 1950.

CITY, KING'S CROSS, HERTFORD, HATFIELD and HITCHIN

WEEKDAYS—continued

THROUGH TRAINS FROM CITY STATIONS, KING'S CROSS OR FINSBURY PARK ARE SHOWN IN BOLD TYPE

A Third Class only.
B Arrives Stevenage 9.43 a.m.
B On Saturdays runs 2 minutes earlier.

FO Fridays only.
FSX Fridays and Saturdays excepted.

SO Saturdays only.
SX Saturdays excepted.

WSO Wednesdays and Saturdays only.
WSX Wednesdays and Saturdays excepted
Y Arrival time.

112.   Here we look north under the elaborate Crescent Road West road bridge, with wagons in the sidings behind the 1884 ground-level timber signal box, and the south portal of Hadley North tunnel in the distance. (Lens of Sutton collection)

113.   This is the view looking towards Hadley South Tunnel. In the 1957-9 quadrupling work, the existing up platform was retained, the down platform was widened into an island for the Fast lines, and a new Down Slow platform was provided on the west side. The old booking office remained at this stage but was later demolished, and a small replacement building provided. All that remains today of the 1885 structures are the two red brick staircases down to the platforms. The station closed to goods in 1950 so no replacement sidings were required at the time of quadrupling. (J.E. Connor collection)

NORTH OF HADLEY WOOD

114.   These two photographs highlight the effects of the quadrupling. Here on 8th April 1959 Class A3 4-6-2 No. 60062 *Minoru* heads the down *Yorkshire Pullman* into Hadley North tunnel on the old Down line, just before the new lines were brought into full use. (J.F. Aylard)

115.   In contrast No. 47523 is seen on 4th September 1978 with an up Cleethorpes service on the same line, which had become the Up Fast on 27th April 1959. (T. Heavyside)

116.   An intermediate signal box was opened between Hadley North and Potters Bar tunnels in 1860, originally named 'Enfield' but renamed 'Ganwick' after the Enfield branch opened. The 1860 box was replaced by the box seen here around 1872. It was set back some way from the running lines and had an unusual rear extension. It was abolished in January 1932 when intermediate colour-light signals were installed in lieu. In this late GNR view 0-8-0 No.417 has just emerged from Potters Bar tunnel with an up coal train. There was another intermediate box, Mimms, located immediately beyond the north end of Potters Bar tunnel, from 1898 to 1922. (The Gresley Society)

Hitchin, Hatfield, Hertford, King's Cross and City — Mondays to Fridays

		B	P	C									P	C	R						C
HITCHIN	d	..	..	0729	0740	0746	..	..	..	..	..	..	..	←	0807	..	..	..	..	..	←
STEVENAGE	d	..	..	36	07a46	53	..	..	..	..	..	0754	..	08a14	0816	..	..	..	..	..	0817
KNEBWORTH	d	..	..	42	→	..	..	..	..	..	..	0800	..	→	..	..	..	..	..	..	23
WELWYN NORTH	d	..	..	47	..	..	..	..	..	..	..	06	..	..	..	..	..	..	..	..	30
WELWYN GARDEN CITY	a	..	..	51	..	..	..	..	..	..	..	10	..	..	..	..	..	..	..	..	34
	d	0747	..	52	..	..	..	..	0803	..	..	11	..	..	0816	..	..	..	..	..	35
HATFIELD	a	..	..	..	..	..	..	..	07	..	..	..	..	..	20	..	..	..	..	..	..
	d	..	..	..	..	..	0755	..	08	..	..	..	..	..	21	..	..	0827	..	..	..
BROOKMAN'S PARK	d	..	..	..	..	..	0800	..	14	..	..	20	..	..	29	..	..	31	..	..	..
POTTERS BAR & SOUTH MIMMS	d	57	..	..	..	..	05	0811	18	..	..	..	..	..	29	..	..	36	..	..	..
HADLEY WOOD	d	..	..	..	..	..	09	14	..	..	..	..	..	..	33	..	..	..	..	..	..
NEW BARNET	d	..	..	..	..	..	12	..	..	..	..	0823	..	..	37	0840	..	41	..	..	..
OAKLEIGH PARK	d	..	..	..	..	..	15	18	..	..	..	25	..	..	..	42	..	..	..	..	..
NEW SOUTHGATE & FRIERN BARNET	d	..	..	..	..	..	19	..	..	..	..	29	..	..	..	0846	..	..	..	..	..
HERTFORD NORTH	d	..	0733	..	..	..	0748	..	..	..	0757	..	..	..	..	..	..	..	0818	..
BAYFORD	d	..	38	..	..	..	53	..	..	..	0802	..	..	..	..	..	..	..	23	..
CUFFLEY & GOFF'S OAK	d	..	44	..	..	..	59	..	..	0804	08	..	..	..	..	0817	..	..	29	..
CREWS HILL	d	..	48	..	..	..	0803	..	..	..	12	..	..	..	..	..	..	..	33	..
GORDON HILL	d	..	51	..	..	0759	..	..	..	09	15	..	..	..	..	22	..	..	..	..
ENFIELD CHASE	d	..	54	..	..	..	08	..	..	12	18	..	..	..	..	25	..	37	..	..
GRANGE PARK	d	..	56	..	..	0802	..	..	..	14	20	..	..	..	..	27	..	..	..	..
WINCHMORE HILL	d	..	59	..	..	05	..	..	..	17	23	..	..	..	..	30	..	..	..	..
PALMERS GREEN & SOUTHGATE	d	..	0802	..	..	..	13	..	..	..	26	..	..	..	..	33	..	42	..	..
BOWES PARK	d	..	..	..	..	09	..	..	..	21	..	..	..	..	..	35	..	..	..	..
WOOD GREEN (ALEXANDRA PARK)	d	..	..	..	..	12	..	..	..	24	..	..	33	..	..	38	..	..	..	..
HORNSEY	d	..	..	..	..	15	..	..	..	27	..	..	36	..	..	..	..	..	..	..
HARRINGAY WEST	d	..	..	..	..	17	..	..	..	..	..	32	38	..	..	42	..	..	..	..
FINSBURY PARK	a	0809	09	0813	..	20	20	26	..	26	30	30	35	41	..	..	45	45	50	50	55
	d	10	10	14	..	21	21	27	..	27	31	32	36	42	..	46	..	46	51	51	56
DALSTON JUNCTION	a	..	..	..	..	34	..	..	41	..	..	49	..	..	..	..	..	58	..
BROAD STREET	a	..	..	..	..	0840	..	..	0847	..	..	0855	..	..	..	..	..	0904	..
YORK ROAD, KING'S CROSS	a	..	08s15	..	..	08s26	..	08s32	..	08s41	..	..	..	..	08s51	..	..	..
KING'S CROSS	a	0816	..	0820	..	0822	..	0827	..	0838	..	0842	..	0847	0852	..	0857	..	0902
KING'S CROSS METROPOLITAN	a	..	s18	..	..	s28	..	s35	..	s44	..	..	..	..	s54	..	..	..
FARRINGDON	a	..	22	..	..	32	..	39	..	48	..	..	..	..	58	..	..	..
BARBICAN	a	..	24	..	..	34	..	42	..	51	..	..	..	..	0900	..	..	..
MOORGATE	a	..	0826	..	..	0836	..	0844	..	0853	..	..	..	..	0902	..	..	..

Extract from the British Rail suburban timetable of 1971

POTTERS BAR

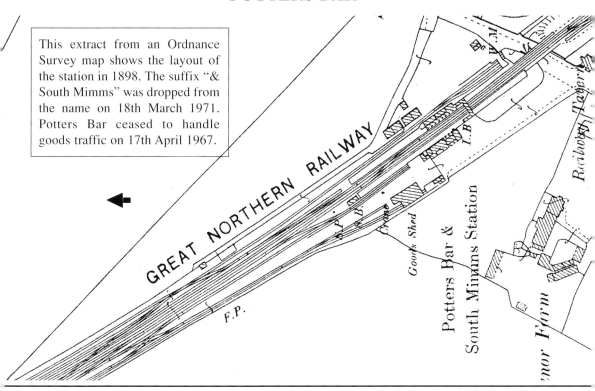

This extract from an Ordnance Survey map shows the layout of the station in 1898. The suffix "& South Mimms" was dropped from the name on 18th March 1971. Potters Bar ceased to handle goods traffic on 17th April 1967.

GREAT NORTHERN RAILWAY

F.P.

Goods Shed

Potters Bar & South Mimms Station

nor Farm

117. Here we see Potters Bar in late Great Northern Railway days. The photographer is standing on the down platform looking north towards the signal box. (The Gresley Society)

118. Potters Bar station remained in its GNR state until work began on quadrupling through the station in 1953. In this 3rd August 1953 view we look south from the signal box steps as a down train arrives. Only the pile of building materials at left hints at the major works just commenced. (D.A. Dant / The Gresley Society)

119. It is now 21st August 1953, and this view north from the footbridge shows serious work in progress on the up side. The old goods yard on the down side is still in use. The famous Class A4 Pacific No. 60014 *Silver Link* is passing through on an up Leeds service. (D.A. Dant / The Gresley Society)

120. This view appears more like a building site than an operating railway station! The original station house and waiting shelters were demolished, and these temporary shelters erected to give some protection for waiting passengers. From beginning to end, the widening works and station rebuilding took two years. Following the completion of the works, the new station was brought into use on 23rd November 1955. The full scope of works included provision of spacious ticket and parcels offices in a new building on the up side. The roadway under Drakes Lane bridge was lowered, allowing headroom of 16ft 6in, as opposed to the rather snug 11ft which had sufficed before. Colour light signalling was installed, controlled from a new signal box at the north end of the up platform. Further photographs of this station appear in the Middleton Press album *Potters Bar To Cambridge*. (D.A. Dant / The Gresley Society)

121. Looking north in 2005, we see a Class 313 electric multiple unit standing at platform 4 whilst working a Moorgate - Welwyn Garden City service. Potters Bar was the scene of an accident on 10th May 2002, when a down train was derailed due to a defective point south of the station, resulting in seven fatalities. (A.C. Mott)

Middleton Press

EVOLVING THE ULTIMATE RAIL ENCYCLOPEDIA

Easebourne Lane, Midhurst, West Sussex.
GU29 9AZ   Tel:01730 813169

www.middletonpress.co.uk   email:info@middletonpress.co.uk

A-978 0 906520 B-978 1 873793 C-978 1 901706 D-978 1 904474 E - 978 1 906008

All titles listed below were in print at time of publication - please check current availability by looking at our website - *www.middletonpress.co.uk* or by requesting a Brochure showing our *LATEST* RAILWAY TITLES also our TRAMWAY, TROLLEYBUS, MILITARY and WATERWAYS series